the **Beefeater**
2-Day Guide
to London by Stephen Bayley

"The chief advantage of London is that a man is always near his burrow."

James Boswell, Life of Johnson (1791)

"One thing, at least, I learnt from my London experience: better a small city where one knows all it has to offer, than a great city where one has no disinterested friend to direct him to the right places to find out what he wants."

Oliver Wendell Holmes, One Hundred Days in Europe (1887)

BLOOMSBURY

First published in 1993 by Bloomsbury Publishing Limited, 2 Soho Square, London W1V 5DE.

The moral right of the author has been asserted.

Text (c) Stephen Bayley 1993

ISBN 0 7475 1516 6

A copy for the CIP entry for this book is available from the British Library.

Design by Perception Design Limited
in association with Scope Communications Management

Typeset by The Graphic Unit

Photographs by Trevor Key

Illustrations by David Holmes

Printed in Italy by Arte Grafica

How to Use This Book

This guide is exclusive, not inclusive. It excludes rubbish and the over-familiar and makes absolutely no claim to comprehensiveness. Rather, it is partial and idiosyncratic, but I hope it is stimulating, interesting and well informed. It is written for the visiting individual, or perhaps couple, with a little time to spare and some money to spend. The idea for writing it arose during melancholy periods in foreign hotel rooms with nothing to do but wait for tomorrow's flight or ferry, wishing to goodness I knew someone who really understood the city and could give me useful indications of how best, depending on the time of day or mood, to spend spare time in a short visit.

While I don't doubt there are places of quality which have been unfortunately excluded, I don't know where they are. Every recommendation in this guide comes from first-hand experience. These are the sort of places I would like to know about when I am abroad. If a famous place is not recommended here, there is a reason. Equally, although some of the entries may be harsh (I prefer to call them realistic), any shop or restaurant mentioned here has real qualities which a discriminating visitor can enjoy, but that is not to say they are perfect. This is a guide book for mature people who have grown out of other guide books. Any visitor who needs to be told to see Buckingham Palace would not find a guide of this subtlety useful. For visitors at that stage of evolution there are plenty of existing guides, and the Yellow Pages.

The restaurant recommendations don't mention specific dishes for two reasons. One, this can raise expectations which are sometimes not satisfied, and two, adds a spurious air of precision. Food is volatile, and a dish that worked well one day may fail the next. Instead, I have tried to give a concise summary of the more poetic and humane reasons to visit a restaurant; food is usually only one part of a larger whole, although in most cases I have tried to hint at the style and quality of the cooking.

Prices are not given, since any declaration in this area invites accusations of inaccuracy. However, warnings are given for exceptionally expensive places. Neither are opening times provided because these often change and, in any case, it is prudent people who will find this guide useful and they are the sort who phone ahead to make reservations.

There is a very useful free service called the Restaurant Switchboard (081-888 8080) which gives phone numbers, opening times and other information about all the establishments listed here. The weekly listings magazine *Time Out* gives a comprehensive survey of temporary events – film, exhibitions, performing arts – covering high-, middle- and low-brow tastes. The *Evening Standard*, whose first edition appears around midday, is indispensable for any permanent or temporary Londoner. BBC's GLR (Greater London Radio) on 94.9FM, is an unusually intelligent local radio station with the best weather, traffic and information services.

Any compact, idiosyncratic guide designed to be used by people on the hoof presents problems of methodology. No great purpose is served here by too zealous or rigid an approach, but it is worth pointing out that in each section there is an unpedantic logic about the sequence of entries, augmented by the quick-reference symbology. So, if you find yourself staying in Chelsea and you want to buy a pair of shoes, you would go to Patrick Cox (see p.64) and then, if you were hungry, you would see that an entry recommending lunch at Como Lario (see p.70) is nearby. After lunch, you may feel like browsing through some antiques and you will see that an adjacent entry suggesting a diversion to Piers von Westenholz (see p.70) is also nearby. But the entries have *not* been rigorously organized street by street: the logic is relaxed, but makes sense. This is a guide you dip into, rather than use from beginning to end.

Introduction

Cities betray the preoccupations of their inhabitants, or perhaps focus them. Maybe there is actually something about a great city's accidents of geography, topography and demography which form national character. Native Londoners are notoriously negligent of their environment, and it is a curious truism that London has been best appreciated by foreigners: the two finest architectural accounts of London are by a Dane and a German, Steen Eiler Rasmussen and Nikolaus Pevsner. Yet, despite the entrenched philistinism of its inhabitants, London is surely the most beautiful and humane big city on earth.

London is one of the planet's four major urban systems, and the least organized. It does not have the vertiginous, hectic, insular brilliance of New York. It does not have the refined elegance of Paris. It does not have the eccentric dynamism of Tokyo. But London does have a collection of qualities, a unique synthesis of shops, restaurants, views, buildings and institutions, an easygoing, informal demeanour, a completeness, which make New York, Paris and Tokyo appear impoverished or limited. There is nowhere else on earth where there is quite so *much to do* as in London. With the sole exceptions of sunbathing and mountaineering, any tastes can be satisfied here, any curiosities gratified, although it has to be admitted that London is not much of a late night city. There are very few restaurants of quality which take bookings after 11.00 pm and late night drinking, despite recent relaxation of licensing laws, takes place in private clubs. London goes to bed well before midnight and visitors, especially those from New York, will be astonished at the almost complete want of smart night-clubs. The one or two where superannuated rock-stars and bloated tycoons are reported by gossip columnists are fiercely members-only; the ones where you pay at the door do not exert much appeal to cultivated people.

Oscar Wilde correctly observed that London has a civilizing influence on its inhabitants and visitors. Even Shakespeare, a country boy, 'wrote nothing but doggerel and lampoon before he came to London and never penned a line after he left'. Samuel Johnson said he could talk twice as much in London as anywhere else. It is extraordinary to reflect on the variety of literature written here: Karl Marx's *Das Kapital* was written in the British Library's Reading Room; Chaucer's *Canterbury Tales* was written in London too, and so was Shaw's *Man and Superman*, Israel Zangwill's *Children of the Ghetto*, Anthony Hope's *The Prisoner of Zenda*, Nathaniel Hawthorne's *The Scarlet Letter*, Thackeray's *Vanity Fair*, Roget's *Thesaurus*, Dr Johnson's *Dictionary*, Jerome K. Jerome's *Three Men in a Boat*, Carlyle's *The French Revolution*, Oscar Wilde's *The Picture of Dorian Gray*, Sir Thomas More's *Utopia*, Ruskin's *The Stones of Venice*, Marlowe's *Dr Faustus*, Shakespeare's *Hamlet*, Defoe's *Robinson Crusoe*, Evelyn Waugh's *Decline and Fall*, Henry James's *What Maisie Knew*, Byron's *The Corsair* and Dickens's *Oliver Twist*.

London is famously a collection of villages, not a city designed on a grid like New York, or to a grand plan like Paris, or hurriedly developed like Tokyo. Even today in the busiest parts of the city, ghosts of old villages are revealed in street patterns. To Dr Johnson London's urban character was not in 'the showy evolutions of buildings, but in the multiplicity of human habitations'. There is something about this haphazard development which is characteristically London. Whether it is a cause or an effect of the famed English diffidence no one can say, but London is a city which does not make *strong* impressions. It has shades rather than colours and lacks characteristic scents and smells. London may be huge – Henry James said it had an 'inconceivable immensity' – but it is also very small. You could spend an entire lifetime in, say, London SW7 – an area of perhaps a square mile – and not be bored by the variety of shops and restaurants, museums and services. Indeed, many Londoners live like this, cultivating fierce loyalty about their own neighbourhoods. A resident of South Kensington regards Chelsea as bohemian and Fulham as positively foreign. Between Hampstead and Belgravia there is no human traffic; each district regards the other as impossibly remote, exotic and irrelevant.

This is a guide for people who don't like or need guide books. It is written by a Londoner for people – either visitors or curious residents – who want to get to know the very best of this city. It is deliberately partial and intimate, but – I believe – deadly accurate. Each entry provides an insider's sample and allows the curious to get to know something a mere tourist would never discover. 'In London,' Boswell wrote in his *Life of Johnson*, 'a man may live in splendid society at one time, and in frugal retirement at another.' London has something for every taste. The *Beefeater 2-Day Guide* tells you what and where. It helps turn London into a small city.

Contents

River Thames

Islington and King's Cross

Covent Garden and Bloomsbury

The City, Docklands and the Southeast

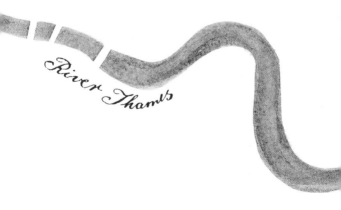

River Thames

Key to symbols

 Place of interest

 Place of architectural interest

 Restaurant

 Hotel

 Place for breakfast

 Place for lunch

 Place for dinner

 Place for a drink

 Place for tea or coffee

 Clothes shop

 Food shop

 Specialist shop

 Bookshop

Antiques and furniture

Museum

Gallery

Library

Hairdresser

Cinema

Body pampering place

An English Classic

Mayfair and West End

This is the most familiar part of London to most visitors. Mayfair – smart, largely residential, very expensive – takes its name from the old fair transferred in the seventeenth century from the Haymarket to what was then the western boundary of the city. Mayfair's western boundary is still clearly defined by Park Lane, the old millionaire's row but now a ferociously busy road separating Mayfair from Hyde Park. The West End is a less specific denomination and suggests that whole area of stores and hotels between Park Lane and Trafalgar Square, Oxford Street and Piccadilly. Traditionally, people "come up West" for exposure to bright lights.

Still, any two day visit to Mayfair and the West End should begin with a pious trip to a modest and sombre curiosity: The Imperial Standards on the north side of Trafalgar Square, between the statues of Admiral Jellicoe and Admiral Cunningham. Here are the definitive measures of the inch, foot and the yard – a small, haunting memorial to past certainties, now lost in modern international metric bustle.

Wallace Collection

Manchester Square London W1M 6BN
Tel 071·935 0687 Fax 071·224 2155

An outstanding collection of British, Dutch, French, Spanish and Flemish paintings, as well as ceramics, arms and armour. Despite the ubiquitous gold on the clocks, the frames, the tooling of the weapons, the setting is on the sombre side of tranquil, a reminder of what museums used to be like. It is a late nineteenth-century *private* collection frozen in time, a snapshot of late Victorian taste. Created by the third Marquess of Hertford (art adviser to the Prince Regent), by the fourth Marquess of Hertford and the latter's son, Sir Richard Wallace, the collection was given to the nation by Lady Wallace in 1897 on the firm understanding that nothing might be added, subtracted, lent, borrowed or acquired. The two outstanding paintings are Frans Hals's *The Laughing Cavalier* (1624) and Fragonard's *The Swing* (1767).

Le Muscadet

25 Paddington Street London W1M 3RF
Tel 071·935 2883

Le Muscadet is in an uninspiring building, but inside is a convincing bistro, the sort which the French do so much better in London than in France. The food is very sound, robust and mercifully unfashionable. Excellent cheeses and service that is intelligently friendly without being either condescending or obsequious.

Efes Kebab House

80 Great Titchfield Street London W1P 7AF
Tel 071·636 1953 Fax 071·636 1953

Turkish food has no better reputation than it deserves. Efes Kebab House, in London's garment district, is very slightly better than most. There is Buzbag Turkish wine and Efespilsen Turkish beer, which travel only fairly well, but if you have a longing for Levantine food in the West End you can do no better. It is quite a fun place.

Royal Institute of British Architects

66 Portland Place London W1N 4AD
Tel 071-580 5533 Fax 071-255 1541

The headquarters of the beleaguered British architects, the
RIBA has a magnificent 1934 building by Grey Wornum, a
beautiful reconciliation of modernism, deco and tradition.
Inside, spaces and materials are superb. The British
Architectural Library is on the fourth floor; it is open to the
public, has brilliantly efficient reference staff and is
altogether one of the best architectural libraries in the world.
Anybody researching buildings past or present *has* to come
here. The ground floor has an excellent bookshop; the
basement has marvellously comfortable, stately lavatories
and phone booths of marble with bronze fittings.

Sagne

105 Marylebone High Street London W1N 3DB
Tel 071-935 6240

A dignified tea and coffee shop, ordinary, but indefinably
smart. Pleasant for breakfast.

Stephen Bull

5-7 Blandford Street London W1H 3AA
Tel 071-486 9696

Stephen Bull is a very good restaurant without being a
specially likeable one. The interior design by Peter Glyn-
Smith (also responsible for L'Incontro in Chelsea) is very
accomplished and photographs well, but is uncomfortable
to sit in and work in, being sharp, cold and hard-edged. In
summer thermal gain makes it unbearable. There is a touch
of megalomania about the place: the paper napkin rings
carry the chef-proprietor's signature, but this is probably
justified as Bull enjoys a good reputation among native
restaurant-goers. The cooking is very modern-eclectic, with
an emphasis on fish; the style is peasant-proletarian, but
put through the mouli of Bull's brain so that it comes out
ultra-refined. A dish described as a hamburger once arrived
as a precarious polychromatic sculptured pyramid. Anyone
wanting to experience some of the best contemporary
British cooking should come here, without necessarily
expecting to enjoy himself. Stephen Bull is an impressive
operation, but a somewhat soulless one.

Villandry Dining Room

89 Marylebone High Street London W1M 3DE
Tel 071-224 3799 Fax 071-486 1370

Just around the corner from Stephen Bull, Villandry makes a remarkable contrast. No personalities here, just ethnic tradition. The Dining Room is behind the shop (which carries a very interesting range of fine French manufactured foods; not a *traiteur*, more a gift and snack shop). It is brilliantly unpretentious, even humble, with hardwood chairs and paper table-cloths, and fundamentally simple dishes. The pleasures of lunch could be defined by a visit to Villandry – a cordial, comfortable environment where all the inhabitants are seriously engaged in the provision or consumption of good food. Close your ears and you could almost be in France.

Hale Clinic

7 Park Crescent London W1N 3HE
Tel 071-631 0156/071-637 3377
Fax 071-323 1693

'Alternative' therapies are now so widespread that it is tempting to consider a dictionary redefinition of the word. The Hale Clinic, in John Nash's majestic Park Crescent, is London's outstanding centre for all forms of 'alternative' treatment.

Vidal Sassoon

56 Brook Street London W1Y 1YB
Tel 071-493 5428

The socially secure will prefer the hairdressing available in Claridge's just opposite; this link in Vidal Sassoon's international chain offers a modernist alternative.

Claridge's

Brook Street London W1A 2JQ
Tel 071-629 8860 Fax 071-499 2210

Claridge's is, with its daily comings-and-goings of the very rich and very famous and their retinues of liveried flunkies and variegated security men, one of the most celebrated hotels in the world. Standards of service and environment are faultless, although some people find it a little stiff and the famous Art Deco interior is muted rather than dramatic. Service in the restaurant is not always civil and the prices are very steep, but the less formal Causerie has a cosmopolitan smorgasbord which is excellent value for lunch. Wonderful lavatories.

Comme des Garçons

59 Brook Street London W1Y 1YE
Tel 071-493 1258

Comme des Garçons, the retail expression of Japanese fashion designer Rei Kawakubo, sometimes seems like revenge for all the insults and humiliations tourists from Tokyo have received from hoity-toity shopkeepers in London, Paris and New York over the years. The interiors are designed with an austerity that makes minimalists wince. Expensive, odd clothes for people influenced by the fashion pages.

St Christopher's Place

St Christopher's Place is a somewhat precious collection of boutiques and attention-seeking cafés in a picturesque alley running between Oxford Street and Wimpole Street. Besides a handful of familiar high street brands are:
Nick and Lulu Rayne 19 St Christopher's Place London W1 Tel 071-935 5589 Fax 071-706 2351 for amusing children's shoes; **Mulberry 11-12 Gees Court St Christopher's Place London W1 Tel 071-493 2546** the showpiece shop of this interesting accessory and country-gentleman-à-la-mode chain; **Pip Hackett 'The Mad Hatter' 21 Barrett Street Street Christopher's Place London W1M 5HP Tel 071-495 3639** eccentric millinery; **Under Two Flags 4 St Christopher's Place London W1M 5HB Tel 071-935 6934** militaria.

Heywood Hill

10 Curzon Street London W1
Tel 071-629 0647 Fax 071-408 0286

One of London's better bookshops, with a large and interesting stock of old and new titles mixed together hugger-mugger. The assistants are knowledgeable and helpful; in fact, they can make you feel a teeny bit coarse. They don't actually ask, 'Can sir read?' but sometimes it feels that way.

George F Trumper

9 Curzon Street London W1Y 7FL
Tel 071-499 1850 Fax 071-281 9337

A traditional hairdresser, who also sells his own antique scents, including Curzon and Essence of Lime. You don't need to have a haircut; the ex-physiotherapist of the Hungarian football team gives head and face massages in the basement. It is all a little too self-conscious nowadays.

Gavroche

43 Upper Brook Street London W1Y 1PF
Tel 071-408 0881 Fax 071-491 4387

The Gavroche is the headquarters of the Roux organization and dynasty, that chain of restaurants and spin-off restaurants belonging to Albert or Michel Roux, their relatives and apprentices. Quite fairly, the Roux brothers (truculent Albert and mischievous Michel) have a reputation for transforming London's expectations of eating over the past twenty or so years. The Gavroche is a restaurant of quite exceptional quality, although one that is in many ways rather dated. The greeting and service are beyond criticism, although some will find the subterranean gloom of the wood panelling and velour a little overpoweringly cute-heritage-claustrophobic and, surely?, there can be no one, anywhere, who is still impressed by *cloches*. The menu is defiantly unfashionable, but superbly executed, although hostile to those still concerned about animal fats; this is a very carnivorous, red-wine, rich reduction sort of restaurant. Gavroche offers food as good as you will find in a similar restaurant in Paris, which is to say the best of its kind in the world. Clientele tends to be morose, muttering millionaires. Wine list is stellar in price and range, although the decent house wine is astonishingly cheap and the *prix fixe* lunch is an amazing bargain.

Pizza on the Park

11 Knightsbridge London SW1X 7LY
Tel 071-235 5550

One of the more spacious of the reliable Pizza Express chain with live jazz. Just opposite Hyde Park, it is a good place for a weekend lunch with children. Parking impossible.

Four Seasons and The Soufflé

**Inn on the Park Hamilton Place
London W1A 4AZ
Tel 071-499 0888 Fax 071-493 1895
Inter Continental 1 Hamilton Place
London W1V 0QY
Tel 071-409 3131 Fax 071-409 7460**

The Four Seasons and the nearby Soufflé are two examples of very fine hotel dining rooms, offering high-quality cooking in surroundings of bizarre hideousness or mimsy pretension. The Four Seasons (cook: Bruno Loubet) has a good view of Hyde Park; the Soufflé (cook: Peter Kromberg) is underground. There is little to choose between the two in terms of quality and presentation, although service at the Soufflé tends to be of the unctuous-Francophone-hustle type, at the Four Seasons more non-specifically international. Each restaurant is comfortable rather than characterful, better suited to a working lunch, with a colleague you admire rather than an intimate dinner with someone you love. Each has a value-for-money *prix fixe* menu for midday.

The Oak Room

**Meridien Hotel 21 Piccadilly London W1V 0BH
Tel 071-734 8000 Fax 071-437 3574**

Here, in far more glamorous surroundings than the Four Seasons and the Soufflé (of what used to be the Piccadilly Hotel – shades of Oscar Wilde), there is a similar standard of cooking on offer, although *accueil* can be cold in this Air France establishment.

Swaine Adeney

**185 Piccadilly London W1V 0HA
Tel 071-734 4277 Fax 071-494 1976**

Now partly owned by Japanese and therefore rather skewed towards new money, Swaine Adeney Brigg maintains its reputation as a provider of saddlery and other accoutrements for horse folk and would-be horsefolk. *The* place to accessorize your Range Rover.

Sotheran

**2 Sackville Street London W1X 2DD
Tel 071-439 6151 Fax 071-434 2019**

Large, old-established, expensive and well-organized antiquarian book and manuscript seller. Especially good on architecture.

Bernard Quaritch

5-8 Lower John Street London W1R 4AU
Tel 071-734 2983 Fax 071-437 6967
One of London's most respected antiquarian booksellers.

Thomas Pink

35 Dover Street London W1X 4AN
Tel 071-493 6775
The Dover Street shop is the most central of this small chain, which sells conservatively cut shirts (and socks, ties and boxer shorts) at non-shocking prices.

The Connaught

Carlos Place London W1Y 6AL
Tel 071-499 7070 Fax 071-495 3262
The difference between the Connaught and the other treasures of the Savoy Group (the Savoy itself and Claridge's) is that while Claridge's tends to be favoured by heads of state and chairmen of the board, and the Savoy attracts figures from showbusiness and politics, the Connaught's customers are *spending their own money*, new or old. This is reflected in the character of the place: it is far more domestic in style and scale than either of its siblings – not unlike a grand country house. The restaurant and Grill Room are among the very best; in fact, there is nowhere better to experience the weighty perfection of Franco-English cooking, with its emphases on plain meats, pies, puddings and stews and its consistently superb service (the waiters can remove and replace a soiled or crumby table-cloth without seeming to disturb you). But the real reason to go to the Connaught is breakfast, a London institution for grown-up media figures, politicians and run-of-the-mill powermongers. Food is classical, but the coffee not as good as you might expect. They do not take bookings. This can be harrowing for the maladroit, but a pleasing game for the regulars. However, the accomplished staff never embarrass visitors – unless they forget their tie.

Church of the Immaculate Conception

Farm Street 14 Mount Street London W1Y 6AH
Tel 071-493 7811
This society-Catholic Jesuit church, just across the road from the Connaught, is where Evelyn Waugh worshipped and harrowed the priests.

John Baily & Sons

116 Mount Street London W1Y 5HD

Tel 071-499 1833

Probably London's oldest butcher and poulterer has been
at this address since 1720.

Hamilton's Gallery

13 Carlos Place Grosvenor Square

London W1Y 5AG

Tel 071-499 9493 Fax 071-629 9919

Next door to the Connaught is this continuous selling
exhibition of celebrity photographers, including David Bailey
and Helmut Newton. Expensive for snaps, but cheap as art.

Maggs

50 Berkeley Square London W1X 6EL

Tel 071-493 7160 Fax 071-499 2007

Bookshops should be the most civilized of shopping
experiences, but too often the failed poets and aspiring
publishers who work behind the counters find a keen
source of pleasure in being off-hand or superior with
customers. Hatchards service can be patchy, assistants
sometimes make you feel you are an irritating nuisance
in their working schedule. But supreme in its ability to
intimidate, even terrify, customers is the awesomely
patrician Maggs of Berkeley Square, whose only
concession to modern times is to be close to Annabel's,
although the idea of crossover trade is laughable. Maggs
has every feature you need to unsettle the insecure,
including staff of ineffable remoteness and other customers
who seem to have been invited, but best of all it does not
actually look like a shop, rather a private house. You feel
very much as though you are crashing a genteel party of
titled ladies with a literary bent. None the less, it's a
marvellous bookstore.

Pizzeria Condotti

4 Mill Street London W1R 9TE

Tel 071-499 1308

Just opposite the famous old Rolls-Royce showroom, this is
the showpiece of the impressive and cheap Pizza Express
chain, which serves quality food at very reasonable prices.
Decent pizza, decent salad, decent wine, decent service,
smartish environment. It is very rare to be able to say it, but

you can *never* go wrong in a Pizza Express establishment. Condotti was decorated (and is co-owned) by Enzo Apicella, the Neapolitan journalist who introduced the trattoria concept to London thirty-five years ago. No booking.

Langan's Brasserie

Stratton Street London W1X 5FD
Tel 071-493 6437

Langan's Brasserie is part of contemporary London folklore. Once the tired old Coq d'Or, it was converted in what seems like another lifetime by the late Peter Langan, the extravagant stage-drunk in crumpled white linen suit, who partnered actor Michael Caine and cook Richard Shepherd in the creation of this unique place. Nearly two decades after opening there is pressure for tables, especially the right tables. Celebrities still come here, but so too do serious locals. Whatever the time of day, the bustle is legendary. Food is not transcendental in its quality, but merely very good and satisfying (although the asparagus soufflé with anchovy sauce is legendary). Prices are unaggressive. Dress up or dress down, but Langan's is not the sort of place to go-as-you-are – it's still a bit special. Insist on a ground-floor table.

Thomas Goode

19 South Audley Street London W1Y 5DN
Tel 071-499 2823 Fax 071-629 4230

Selling glass and china to the aristocracy and gentry since 1845, Goode's preserves the feel of a nineteenth-century department store. There are two fabulous Minton ceramic elephants by the entrance. The store includes a franchise of **Ken Turner**, London's best florist.

James Purdey & Sons

57 South Audley Street London W1Y 6ED
Tel 071-499 1801 Fax 071-355 3297

Purdey is, like Ferrari and Château Yquem, an absolute – one of those products (in this case handmade shotguns) which defines itself and has no peers. Among the fishing and shooting set, the feeling is that Purdey is rather more old money than its rival, **Holland & Holland**
13 Bruton Street London W1X 7DD
Tel 071-499 4411 Fax 071-499 4544, which is almost imperceptibly more vulgar.

Harry's Bar

26 South Audley Street London W1Y 5DJ
Tel 071-408 0844 Fax 071-491 1474

Harry's Bar is actually a private club, run by the proprietor of
Annabel's, the nightclub favoured by middle-aged ravers.
Here the very rich and their friends, the limo folk, can eat
excellent Venetian food and not be disturbed by the sight of
poor people.

The area called **Shepherd Market** recalls the rustic old
May Fair, although there is nothing pastoral about it today.
Nowadays it is full of patchy restaurants, quality souvenir
shops, pubs selling food described as 'fayre', ironmongers
and specialist sexual therapy advisers (with some very
famous clients). The more attractive parts include the

**Curzon Cinema Curzon Street London W1Y 7AF
Tel 071-465 8865** with the most comfortable cinema
seats in London, always showing films of quality, and the

**Al Hamra 31-33 Shepherd Market London
W1Y 7RJ Tel 071-493 1954** one of the best Lebanese
restaurants in the city, which is not saying much because
many of the others are life threatening, but Al Hamra offers
convincing authenticity and accomplished service.

Dorchester Hotel

Park Lane London W1A 2HJ
Tel 071-629 8888 Fax 071-409 0114

The Dorchester is one of the very grandest hotels in the
world, an original Art Deco masterpiece, recently
refurbished with perhaps too much zeal by the Sultan of
Brunei. Some wags say he bought it as his London *pied-à-
terre*. For austere tastes The Dorchester is nowadays a bit
overdone, a bit clamorous and a bit too conscious of its
celebrity. The limo crowd leave their drivers and barges
outside; ordinary people may find parking a problem. There
are three restaurants: The Grill (generally British), The
Terrace (Franco-international) and The Oriental (Sino-
international). The Dorchester is calm, accomplished and
has very few surprises. The Grill is a sophisticated breakfast
rendezvous for people who need sophistication at breakfast
time.

The Greenhouse

27A Hay's Mews London W1X 7RJ
Tel 071-499 3331 Fax 071-225 0011

Now under the same management as Knightsbridge's Capital Hotel and with a celebrity chef installed, this Mayfair institution is in a backwater between Berkeley Square and Park Lane. It is the sort of restaurant that attracts regular customers, in this case local business people of a conservative disposition who tend to wear dark suits every season. The cooking is a sensitive interpretation of English standards: mashed potatoes, faggots, boiled ham and so forth, but made contemporary with continental trims, including aioli and plum tomatoes (though not on the same dish). The prices are easygoing and there is a busy atmosphere. The Greenhouse feels like a super-sophisticated canteen for upper management.

Anderson & Sheppard

30 Savile Row London W1X 1AG
Tel 071-734 1420 Fax 071-734 1721

Savile Row is the Valhalla of English snobbery. Nowhere on earth are there so many jumped-up tradesmen pretending to be gentlemen, fuelled by the high-octane experience of daily encounters with the inside legs of aristocrats and royals. Close contact with ducal and princely bodies has helped Savile Row institute a culture of disdain for ordinary folk. This was briefly interrupted by the glorious vulgarity of Tommy Nutter, but after his death Savile Row will return to type. All the tailors have long traditions and each cultivates the feel of a *club privé*, but first among equals in this craft of lofty exclusivity is Anderson & Sheppard. Only the very confident or the foolhardy but armour-plated would visit without an appointment or an introduction. Atmosphere apes a country house, but is closer to an expensive dentist's waiting room. A tradition of gentlemen never paying their tailors makes Anderson & Sheppard insensitive to the clamour of the marketplace.

Philip Kingsley

54 Green Street London W1Y 1RH
Tel 071-629 4004 Fax 071-491 9843

An admired hairdresser.

South Molton Street used to be known as Poverty Lane, but now accommodates **Browns 23-27 South Molton Street London W1Y 1DA Tel 071-491 7833 Fax 071-408 1281** London's best collection of high-fashion women's ready-to-wear. There is an adjacent male Brown's, but it appeals to a more limited market. Around the back of Brown's is the confusing and very patchy **Gray's Antique Market 58 Davies Street London W1 Tel 071-629 7034**, too close to the sewer of Oxford Street to be a pleasure. Back in South Molton Street the **Electrum Gallery 21 South Molton Street London W1Y 1DD Tel 071-629 6325** has an interesting selection of modern craftsman jewellery and is staffed by people who seem to enjoy their work and try to be helpful.

Molton Brown

58 South Molton Street London W1Y 1HH Tel 071-629 1872 (women)/071-493 5236 (men)
The flavour in this diversified hairdresser is a little bit 1970s, but not unstylish.

In *Afterthoughts* (1931) American Bloomsburyite Logan Pearsall Smith wrote: 'I like to walk down Bond Street, thinking of all the things I don't want.' It is still a bit like that today – an embarrassment of riches.

Yves Saint Laurent

New Bond Street London W1Y 9FA Tel 071-493 0405 Fax 071-495 0205
The London branch of the French empire. Time-travel interior design, directly reminiscent, like the logo, of Paris discos of the early 1970s and the era of velvet suits worn with tank tops. Buying Yves Saint Laurent has never made much sense in the British market, unless you want period costume for driving your Citroën-Maserati.

Ralph Lauren

143 New Bond Street London W1 Tel 071-491 4967 Fax 071-409 2603
The London branch of the American empire. At Ralph Lauren a commissionaire opens the door for the Japanese customers and gives the maladroit a martial stare. It is extremely difficult to distinguish the staff from the customers

as they are all united by a taste for Gatsby costume dramas. 'Nessun Dorma' plays, while fretful customers dither between the merchandise and the propping.

Gianni Versace

34 Old Bond Street London W1X 3AE
Tel 071-499 1862 Fax 071-499 1719

Of the two great names in contemporary Italian fashion, **Armani Sloane Street** is a distinguished designer who trades with nicely understated taste. Versace is like an explosion in a toy factory, a purveyor of offensive gaudy costumes, to the misguided rich. Ten years too late Versace has chosen London as the flagship store in his vulgar global empire. The style is an indescribable nightmare mishmash of glam rock and Marie-Antoinette, as if they had turned the Crillon Hotel into MTV. There is *trompe l'oeil* and marble, and you marvel at the ability, at this stage in evolution, to conceive something so hopelessly out of touch with the tenor of the times. Exquisite staff stand around with absolutely nothing to do, waiting for the beginning of a movie that is late starting to roll.

Rayne

15 Old Bond Street London W1X 3DB
Tel 071-493 9077 Fax 071-495 2330

A shoe and handbag maker since 1889, the scriptural home of the court shoe, the favoured footwear supplier of the Queen.

Waddington Galleries

10 Cork Street London W1X 1PD
Tel 071-437 8611 Fax 071-734 4146

Fine art was at its best when it was a commodity. In the Middle Ages, even in the Renaissance, great religious pictures were items of trade as much as exaltation. Try telling that to an assistant in a smart West End gallery, such as Waddington, and they take pride in basilisk stares which make you feel a jerk. Waddington's in Cork Street, despite the dire condition of the art market, preserves the air of a bogus cathedral or semi-exclusive club where membership is acquired by cash not by taste. The staff like to let you know that, but try to remember it is just a shop selling fine art. Artists in Waddington stock include most of the art-critic-approved modernists. Most of the prices are in Swiss bank territory, although some graphic works are for sale at hundreds rather than millions.

Belvoir & Watson

15 Cork Street London W1
Tel 071-491 0681

Interesting small jeweller.

Alistair McAlpine

33 Cork Street London W1X 1HB
Tel 071-437 4760 Fax 071-494 3854

One of the most extraordinary shops in London, an eighteenth-century cabinet of curios assembled *for sale* with fanatical eccentricity by Mrs Thatcher's closest confidant and author of the Machiavelli parody *The Servant*. Possibly the only place in London where you can buy an Egyptian mummy.

Suntory

72 St James's Street London SW1A 1PH
Tel.071-409 0201 Fax 071-499 7993

The grandest of London's Japanese restaurants and appropriately sombre. The menu has chef's suggestions, which sometimes breech the envelope of Japanese kitchen conventions. Suntory caters for heavy yen business, so dining is expensive. There are few private diners. A must for visitors in need of a periodic fix of authentic Japanese sobriety and a whiff of Tokyo expenses. A short cab ride away **Isohama 312 Vauxhall Bridge Rd London SW1V 1AA Tel 071-834 2145** offers a rougher version of Japanese cooking at very friendly prices in an environment like an upholstered garage.

The Square

32 King Street London SW1Y 6RJ
Tel 071-839 8787 Fax 071-321 2124

Perhaps because the old clubs dominate the area, St James's is curiously lacking quality restaurants. The Square is the most successful restaurant ever to appear on one of those city sites that seems strangely doomed and has hitherto hosted desperate varieties of bad Italian and faux-sophisticated French places. Decoration by David Collins is in a challenging style not known to art historians, but somewhat reminiscent of a mid-1950s' Swedish exhibition on interior design. It is very bright and colourful and so are the customers; dark blue suits, knitted silk ties, florid faces and plummy voices predominate. Cooking is carefully robust – high-class peasant. The wine list is priced for those who have not just made a fortune at nearby Christies'. If you were assessing this restaurant at a catering school, you would commend the cooking, the service and the prices, but withhold some praise from the ambience. This is not to say it is in any way unpleasant, but it is somehow unrelaxing; impossible to imagine settling down to a bibulous harangue here – everybody is too self-conscious.

In St James's Square (where Nancy Astor, the first woman MP, lived at number 4) is **The London Library 14 Street James's Square London SW1Y 4LB Tel 071-930 7705 Fax 071-930 0436**. Founded by Thomas Carlyle, the London Library is the finest private literary library in Britain. Much used by authors who have mastered the quixotic cataloguing system and by other authors who enjoy a nap after lunch, The London Library is not open to the public, but the privilege of using the evocative, relaxing, learned spaces in the building is worth the cost of membership alone. Apply for a tour at the desk if there is some prospect of your becoming a member. The London Library sends books abroad.

This is clubland: **Boodle's 28 St James's Street London SW1A 1HJ Tel. 071-930 7166; White's 37 St James's Street London SW1A 1JG Tel 071-493 6671; Brooks' St James's Street London SW1A 1LN Tel 071-493 4411 and The Carlton 69 St James's Street London SW1A 1PJ Tel 071-493 1164**. A fine architectural and social counterpoint is Peter and Alison Smithson's **Economist Building 25 St James's Street London SW1A 1JG Tel 071-839 7000**, a concrete-framed Brutalist structure of 1964 which shows how well the language of Modernism works when handled by intelligent architects in the pay of generous clients who care about building maintenance. The little piazza is the only part of London resembling New York at its best. The Smithsons said their grail in architecture was 'ordinariness and light'; here it is, confident and elegant. **The Economist Bookshop Portugal Street London WC2A 2AB Tel 071-405**

5531 Fax 071-430 1584 carries all this successful publisher's titles.

St James's has a tight little group of some of the most singular and inimitable shops in London: **Lock 6 St James's Street London SW1A 1EF Tel 071-930 5849 Fax 071-976 1908** the hatter; **Lobb 9 St James's Street London SW1A 1EE Tel 071-930 3664** the shoemaker; **Harris 29 Street James's Street London SW1A 1HA Tel 071-930 3915 Fax 071-925 2691** the pharmacist; and the much more recent, but still charming and fascinating, **Hugh Johnson 68 St. James's Street London SW1 Tel 071-491 4912 Fax 071-493 0602**, the shop where the world's best-known wine personality sells cultivated drinking accessories.

Nearby are two of London's best wine merchants: **Justerini & Brooks 61 St James's Street London SW1A 1LY Tel 071-493 8721 Fax 071-499 4653**, and the patrician, but superbly gentlemanly and helpful **Berry Bros & Rudd 3 St. James's Street London SW1A 1EG Tel 071-396 9600 Fax 071-396 9611**. The Berry Bros' shop is a marvellous survival of the eighteenth century and the staff retain the courtly manners of a more civilized, if imaginary, era. From their superb list they will give you as much attention and courtesy if you are buying a single bottle of their (incidentally delicious) 'Good Ordinary Claret' (£4.20) or a case of Mouton-Rothschild (£840).

Facing St James's Palace and dating from 1627, Inigo Jones's **Queen's Chapel Marlborough House Marlborough Road London SW1** was the first English church in the Italianate classical style. It is very beautiful, but often closed.

Duke's Hotel

35 St James' Place London SW1A 1NY Tel 071-491 4840 Fax 071-493 1264

This is one of London's most discreet grand hotels, in a very quiet backwater off St James'. The dining room is hushed and intimate and there is a very fine small bar where the barman has won *The Sunday Times*' award for

the best martini. Its neighbour **The Stafford Hotel
16-18 St James's Place London SW1A 1NJ
Tel 071-493 0111 Fax 071-493 7121** has the same
characteristics: its guests ooze understated influence and
emanate category-warping levels of self-confidence. These
are hotels favoured by the very powerful, the very rich and
the very secure. The Stafford has interesting, vast cellars
which can be seen on request.

Quaglino's

**16 Bury Street London SW1Y 6AL
Tel 071-930 6767 Fax 071-839 2866**

In his second coming as London's most impressive
celebrity-restaurateur, it is hard to imagine what Sir
Terence Conran will do after Quaglino's. This astonishing
space, a landmark nightspot from the thirties through to
the sixties, was neglected for sixteen years until Conran
bought it in 1990. It has now been turned into London's
most surprising restaurant, a vast (four hundred seat)
amalgam of food, drink, interior art and design. Every
artifice has been employed. Some may find the self-
consciously hard-edged sybaritic environment a touch
contrived, even overwhelming, but it would be a dull
person who was unamused by cigarette girls in mesh
tights and flouncy skirts, or by the angled mirror above the
shelfwood bar where staff shucking oysters make a *tableau
vivant* for the entire restaurant. Smarter than La Coupole,
more sophisticated than L'Odeon or Luxembourg,
Quaglino's is unique and exciting. Menu is reasonably
priced and unclassifiably eclectic; the restaurant takes very
late orders and on Fridays and Saturdays there is dancing
until three in the morning.

Prestat

**14 Prince's Arcade London SW1Y 6DS
Tel 071-629 4838 Fax 071-408 0124**

In an elegant and slightly over-developed arcade between
Piccadilly and Jermyn Street, is one of the Queen's
favoured chocolate suppliers. The Napoleon Truffles are
famous.

The Bird and Wildlife Bookshop

2-4 Prince's Arcade London SW1Y 6DS
Tel 071-287 1407 Fax 0234 741310

The Bird and Wildlife Bookshop publishes a 52-page guide
of books in print on its subject. Assistants can help with
enquiries about the Black Racket-tailed Tree Pie.

Wiltons

55 Jermyn Street London SW1Y 6LX
Tel 071-629 9955 Fax 071-495 6233

If you buy your shoes at Lobb's (£600 and up), you eat your
grouse and turbot at Wiltons. Jermyn Street is perhaps the
dead centre of urban England and Wiltons feeds it. The
quality of the fish and game is the best, the preparation the
most simple. If you feel you are never, ever going to be
invited to a great country house, go to Wiltons. The food is
better, the furnishing newer, but the ambience essentially
and unalterably English.

Czech & Speake

39c Jermyn Street London SW1Y 6DN
Tel 071-439 0216 Fax 071-734 8587

The exotic name is a marketeer's recent fabrication. Some
find this fragrance specialist too precious, but the
merchandise is powerfully expressive of luxury either as a
personal indulgence or a noteworthy gift. Aromas are
strong.

Alfred Dunhill

30 Duke Street London SW1Y 6DL
Tel 071-499 9566 Fax 071-499 6471

The tobacconist has enlarged into a diversified luxury
goods company, which also owns Mont Blanc pens and
Chloe couture. The St James's headquarters, entrance
opposite Fortnum & Mason's Fountain Restaurant (a decent
place to breakfast if you can tolerate the overbearing
fussiness of the staff at that time of day) is a glossily
modernized temple of luxo-hedonism, not much favoured
by Londoners. After a great deal of successful and costly
evolution into blazers and travel goods, Dunhill's best
products are still its first ones: pipes and lighters.

Harvie & Hudson

77 & 97 Jermyn Street London SW1Y 6NP & 6JE
Tel 071-930 3949 Fax 071-839 7020

More authentic in that they are less disposed to cater for credulous, spendthrift tourists than Turnbull & Asser. Harvie & Hudson is a shirtmaker, but can dress the entire man in English upper middle-class uniform. Neither in the character of its fine quality menswear (from socks to overcoats through shoes and night attire, including fabulous nightshirts) nor in the wonderfully backward retail environment does Harvie & Hudson make any concessions to modernism. This is what buying clothes in the early 1950s was like.

Turnbull & Asser

71 & 72 Jermyn Street London SW1Y 6PF
Tel 071-930 0502 Fax 071-930 9032

Turnbull & Asser, supplier of the Prince of Wales's distinctive shirts and ties, is the best known of the Jermyn Street outfitters and, perhaps, the one most ill affected by the tinselly rash of marketing-based modernization which was prevalent in the 1980s. Still, the shop has a fine selection of generously cut silk ties, distinctive shirts and dressing gowns.

New & Lingwood

53 Jermyn Street London SW1Y 6LX
Tel 071-493 9621 Fax 071-499 3103

New & Lingwood is the Jermyn Street outfitter that has established a style and reputation distinct by several shades of nuance from both Harvie & Hudson and Turnbull & Asser. In a sense the outfitter with the most exclusive reputation (it is the official Eton outfitter), New & Lingwood became a *succès de curiosité* when a generation which was not old Etonian discovered the charm of its slightly rakish style.

Paxton & Whitfield

93 Jermyn Street London SW1Y 6JE
Tel 071-930 0250

A superb, old-fashioned cheese shop, especially good in British types.

Foster & Son

83 Jermyn Street London SW1Y 6JD
Tel 071-930 5385 Fax 071-839 3803
Established in 1840 as a maker of hunting boots, Foster
now makes fine leatherware.

Davidoff

35 St James's Street London SW1A 1HD
Tel 071-930 3079 Fax 071-930 5887
The London headquarters of Zino Davidoff's tobacco
empire, a little showy. Down the road is **Lewis 19 St
James's Street London SW1 Tel 071-930 3787
Fax 071-495 0097**, another tobacconist, nicely
understated.

Burlington Arcade is a Regency mall of thirty-eight
shops, designed by Samuel Ware and built by Lord George
Cavendish in 1819, which runs between Piccadilly and
Burlington Gardens, next door to the Royal Academy. An
interesting architectural and social curiosity, it is by now a
little too self-aware of its duties to tourism to be completely
convincing as a living commercial entity, but still contains
some special shops, including: **Berk 46 Burlington
Arcade London W1V 9AE Tel 071-493 0028
Fax 071-499 4312** for cashmere, shoes and
aristocratic slippers; **W & H Gidden 1-2 Burlington
Arcade London W1V 9AB Tel. 071-495 3670**
for saddlery; **N Peal 37 Burlington Arcade
London W1V 9AE Tel 071-493 5378** for cashmere;
**Michael Sutty 62 Burlington Arcade London
W1V 9AE Tel 071-495 3099** for model soldiers.
At the north end, in Burlington Gardens, **James
J Fox 2 Burlington Gardens London W1X 2JT
Tel 071-493 9009 Fax 071-495 0097** is a
well-stocked cigar merchant.

Caprice

**Arlington House Arlington Street London
SW1A 1RT Tel 071-629 2239 Fax 071-493 9040**
The Caprice is one of London's great restaurants, a place
where shocking pink-faced and black-clad fashion PRs go
to have a smashing glass of champagne with a 'girlfriend'.
Almost impossible to get a table without a reservation, the
Caprice pleases because it is wonderfully smart and buzzy,

but entirely without pretence or affectation. Food is good, simple, not tricksy, and very, very reasonably priced. The service is immaculate and the room itself interesting. If you can take your eyes off the customers, you'll see that Eva Jiricna's tense black and white and metal interior is relieved by classic David Bailey photographs. Good for late supper, Sunday brunch.

The Ritz

Piccadilly London W1V OBR
Tel 071-493 8181 Fax 071-493 2687

The Ritz, or perhaps simply tea at the Ritz, is a mythologized London tradition. Certainly, it is not something familiar to Londoners, but still, the Ritz is special. A fake French château by Edwardian pasticheurs, Mewes and Davis, the Ritz was built in 1906. The street arcade is a deliberate evocation of Paris's rue de Rivoli to enforce suggestions of the fashionable Frenchness. The gilt dining room has a fine view of Green Park. The Ritz is the least demanding and the *quietest* of London hotels, but better for a discreet cocktail than a cucumber sandwich.

Banqueting House

Whitehall London SW1A 2ER
Tel 071-930 4179

One of London's first and finest renaissance palaces, built for King James I by Inigo Jones between 1619 and 1622, the only significant part of the old Whitehall Palace to survive the fire of 1698. Magnificent painted ceiling by Rubens.

Westminster Cathedral

Ambrosden Avenue London SW1P 1QW
Tel 071-834 7452

This is London's Roman Catholic cathedral, designed in a free-and-easy Byzantine style by J.F. Bentley. Begun in 1894, it is not yet finished, something open to different interpretations. It is said that the campanile houses a relic in the form of St John the Baptist's armpit; certainly, there is a curiously evocative feeling about the cathedral and its piazza (especially when compared to the noisy gutter of nearby Victoria Street, a sort of Third World version of Manhattan's Seventh Avenue). Inside, ignoring the mawkish Catholic clutter, the blackened brick domes are magnificent, as are a frieze by Eric Gill and Ernest Gimson's 1912 choir stalls.

Westminster Abbey is perhaps too familiar and too crowded, but **Westminster Abbey Museum London SW1P 3PA Tel 071-222 5152** is a marvellous short cut. In the tastefully converted Norman undercroft of 1070 is an astonishing range of funeral effigies, including King Henry VII, King William III, Queen Mary II, Prime Minister William Pitt and Lord Nelson (which shows him with the wrong blind eye). Here history comes dead.

Cabinet War Rooms

Clive Steps King Charles Street London SW1A 2AQ Tel 071-930 6961

This is a time-capsule jewel of a museum, the bunker beneath the Foreign Office whence Churchill and his Government ran the British version of the Second World War.

St John's Smith Square

London SW1P 3HA
Tel 071-222 2168

A fine and very grand baroque church by Wren's talented assistant Thomas Archer. The interior was destroyed by bombing, but is now used for regular lunchtime concerts of exceptional quality. In the crypt is a better-than-average wine bar called The Footstool. Political voyeurs can watch Tory fat cats sleaze in and out of Conservative Party headquarters in the corner of Smith Square. Lord North Street, running off to the northwest, is perhaps Britain's outstanding political street. For a dose of the flavour of intrigue, privilege and religion in this special area of the capital, read C.P. Snow's *The Corridors of Power*.

Goring Hotel

15 Beeston Place Grosvenor Gardens London SW1W OJW
Tel 071-396 9000 Fax 071-834 4393

This is a rare example of a major hotel still in private hands. Exceptional service and ambience. The dining room presents traditional English food, especially game, with great clarity and attention to detail. Very good wine list with some top quality clarets. The Goring dining room has a splendid atmosphere of understated opulence. People who *know* often dine here.

Tate Gallery

Millbank London SW1P 4RG
Tel 071-821 1313

The Tate Gallery was once as famous for its restaurant with Rex Whistler murals and celebrated wine list with anachronistic pricing as it was for its art collection. But while the Whistlers remain, the cellar has been sold off and replaced with wines more suitable to the very mediocre food, winsomely English. The Tate struggles, not always successfully, to combine the dual roles of being both the national collection of British art *and* the national gallery of modern art. A recent re-hang has, not without controversy, freshened the display and made certain aspects of the collections more accessible at the expense of others. There are singular treasures: Mark Rothko's haunting 'Seagram Murals', painted for New York's Four Seasons restaurant, perhaps being the single most articulate silent witness to the power of abstraction. The Clore wing was designed in confrontational angularity and gaudy polychrome by the late Sir James Stirling, and opened in 1987. It houses the Turner Bequest, but is more a monument to the ego of the architect and patron than to the genius of the artist. Turner and his champion, Ruskin, had wanted his larger pictures, hung in a single room the better to appreciate the enormities and subtleties. Architect and client ignored this interesting idea and pandered to curatorial, art-historical vanities at the expense of public enjoyment and appreciation. Millbank was the site of the notorious Millbank prison (1816–90). Until 1867 prisoners sentenced to transportation began their journey to Australia here.

A short walk from the Tate Gallery is an exceptional Victorian church, **St James-the-Less Moreton Street London SW1** by George Edmund Street, architect and, like so many of his contemporaries but so unusual today, scholar. Street, author of *Gothic Architecture in Spain*, designed everything in this gloriously polychrome red-brick church. A few minutes here and you can feel the intoxicating sense of creativity rather than revivalism which informed the greatest Victorian architects. Nearby is Warwick Way, with a selection of semi-charming, but undistinguished, restaurants, as varied in their ethnicity as Street's architecture, but of less lasting value.

Soho

Soho, described by John Galsworthy in *The Forsyte Saga* as "untidy, full of Greeks, Ishmaelites, cats, Italians, tomatoes, restaurants, organs, coloured stuffs, queer names" retains a strong village character. It is London's centre for drinking clubs, Chinese restaurants, blue movies, old-fashioned vice and new-fashioned cooking. Some establishments combine both. The spine is Old Compton Street, with Greek Street, Frith Street and Dean Street running off it. Here is an extraordinary wealth of good delis, good and bad restaurants, dangerous pubs, exceptional newsagents and eccentric electrical retailers. There are few noteworthy architectural monuments, but Meard Street is unspoiled Georgian and the first floor brothels remain. Dr Johnson knew a resident "generally slut and drunkard, occasionally whore, thief". Busy day and night. Parking impossible.

Frith Street Gallery

60 Frith Street London W1V 5TA
Tel 071-494 1550 Fax. 071-287 3733

In this small gallery Jane Hamlyn specializes in works on paper.

dell'Ugo

56 Frith Street London W1V 5TA
Tel 071-734 8300 Fax 071-734 8784

The proprietor of dell'Ugo energetically opens restaurants and treats them like theatres. Perhaps one day they may even go dark with customers still inside them. dell'Ugo is an extravagant reminder of mid-1980s' flighty extravagance, but the menu is pure early '90s' robust eclectic (with lots of chargrilling and modish vernacular ingredients such as lentils and polenta) and clearly beyond the day-to-day competence of the kitchen. Staff immediately tell you not what is 'special', but what is 'off'. It is difficult to order a well-balanced meal – everything comes with carbohydrate: potatoes, pasta, pulses. But dell'Ugo (which is named after an olive oil) can be amusing for a noisy supper. Muzak catering.

Chiang Mai

48 Frith Street London W1V 5TE
Tel 071-437 7444 Fax 081-985 1767

Vatcharin Bhumichitr, now an author, cooks northern Thai specialities, including a type of fermented pork sausage thought to be illegal under EC regulations. The dishes vary between dramatically hot and interesting, or dismayingly pallid. Co-owner is David Sweetman, the biographer of Van Gogh. Chiang Mai is somewhat seedy, but not inexpensive. Awful wine, but good Thai beer and Thai whisky. Not a specially romantic or charming restaurant, simply one that has made its name by serving good food.

Ronnie Scott's

47 Frith Street London W1V 6HT
Tel 071-439 0747 Fax 071-437 5081

Ronnie Scott, himself a long surviving saxophonist, runs London's favourite jazz club...for the sort of people who have favourite jazz clubs. It is in a dark Soho basement with the usual accessories of smoke and expensive drinks, but it is *the* place where the best acts turn up when in London.

Est

54 Frith Street London W1V 5TE
Tel 071-437 0666

If Giorgio Armani designed a new Italian café, it would be like this. Every fashionable ingredient is on the menu: salsa, polenta, bits of burnt rosemary everywhere and chargrills difficult to avoid. Hard, cramped seating; pleasant food for a quick lunch.

Alastair Little

49 Frith Street London W1V 5TE.
Tel 071-734 5183

Alastair Little is a punishingly uncomfortable restaurant environment: brutish modernistic chairs, painfully unflattering lighting, hard edges and no concessions to comfort and humour (except that you can see the chef and his brigade at work). There is so little to say in favour of the restaurant as an environment that it is just as well that the cooking is usually superb. Inventive combinations with clearly defined flavours create memorable meals, but not a place for intimacy or romance.

Bar Italia

22 Frith Street London W1V 5TS
Tel 071-437 4520

The Bar Italia is closed for one hour a day and, irrespective of what the clock is doing, the other twenty-three are populated by satellite television of Italian football or heavyweight boxing played behind a continuous stream of opera. It is a standing-room only sort of place; coffee is good, but not all that great, but with an institution like the Bar Italia that is not really the point.

French House Dining Rooms

49 Dean Street London W1V 5HL
Tel 071-437 2799

The French House is a pub made famous by journalism. Once the only place in London you could buy lethal *absinthe*, it has become an awful parody of itself; hard-drinking Soho regulars have been all but replaced by a must-see crowd. Upstairs is altogether different. A talented and enterprising pair of very young chefs, Fergus Henderson and Margot Clayton, have converted the grim old dining room into a small restaurant of workmanlike *chic*, with coarse, but delicious, food. It is inexpensive, cramped and service can be hilariously anarchic, but as a dining experience French House may be the last romantic spot in Soho.

Pizza Express

10 Dean Street London W1V 5RL
Tel 071-439 8722

A regular Pizza Express establishment, but with good live jazz.

Au Jardin des Gourmets

5 Greek Street London W1V 5LA
Tel 071-437 1816 Fax 071-437 0043

An ancient monument of Soho, recently refurbished. This is a very *proper* restaurant, absolutely everything is *comme il faut*; the atmosphere is so correct that it would be incongruous to make any dramatic claims, although the wine list (which includes a 1945 Haut-Brion) is exceptional. The food is traditional, with a very slightly modern feel. Au Jardin des Gourmets is a perfect rendezvous for a meal of discretion.

Gay Hussar

2 Greek Street London W1V 6NB
Tel 071-437 0973

Increasing political correctness has not tempted the new proprietors to change the name of this famous, semi-Hungarian restaurant, once favoured by Labour Party gourmands. The menu never changes and makes absolutely no concessions to modernism; more bluntly it tends towards the indigestible with lots of goose, paprika and dumplings, but clearly exercises a very strong appeal to the regulars of whom there are very, very many. Although recently refurbished, the new interior follows exactly the lines and forms of the old: burgundy velour banquettes, lots of framed pictures and dark wood. A wonderful place for a very long lunch on a rainy day (you drink Tokaj with pudding), or a gossipy dinner for two.

I Camisa & Son

61 Old Compton Street London W1V 5PN
Tel 071-437 7610

Time was when Soho was the source of most interesting retail food in London, a village of gastro-erotica. Most old

Soho specialists say that Camisa is *the* best Italian delicatessen, although **Lina Stores 18 Brewer Street London W1R 3FS Tel 071-437 6482** has its devotees. Fact is, both are fine, but in the past ten years gastronomic literacy has so increased that nowadays there is any number of other shops, even some suburban shops, to rival them. In any case, Balducci's or Dean & De Luca in New York make Camisa and Lina look provincial.

Patisserie Valerie

44 Old Compton Street London W1V 5PB Tel 071-437 3466

On the face of it there is no rational reason why Patisserie Valerie is such an astonishing success; its cakes and coffee are no better than they should be, the seating is uncomfortable and crowded, and the 'service' a mockery of the concept, but Soho is the sort of place which attracts enthusiasts and Patisserie Valerie is a place they enthuse about. Watch them jostling in the perspiration and ruffled broadsheet newspapers any weekday morning.

Janet Fitch

25 Old Compton Street London W1V 5PL Tel 071-287 3789

This Old Compton Street shop is an evolution from Janet Fitch's original West Soho shop (which still exists at 2 Percy Street). There are too many embarrassing knick-knacks, but some of the most interesting jewellery in London is often to be found here.

Algerian Coffee Stores Ltd

52 Old Compton Street London W1V 6PB Tel 071-437 2480 Fax 071-437 5470

Besides an exceptional range of beans and blends (Gourmet Noir is a favourite), this Soho institution (founded 1887) sells coffee additives, including roasted and ground chicory, figs, cardamoms and Arabic spices, as well as every method of making coffee. The best place in London to buy an *ibrik*.

Selectadisc (London) Ltd

34-35 Berwick Street London W1V 3RF Tel 071-734 3297 Fax 071-734 3298

An exceptionally well-stocked and rather beat-up and bohemian record store for pop, rock and jazz.

Daniel Field

8-12 Broadwick Street London W1V 1FH
Tel 071- 430 8223 Fax 071-734 2204

Organic and mineral hairdressing.

Ally Capellino Shop

95 Wardour Street London W1V 3TE
Tel 071-494 0768

Ally Capellino's name is a fabrication; she is English, but nowadays it is sometimes advantageous to appear Italian in the fashion business. Capellino sells generously cut, smart-informal menswear and womenswear.

Thomas Sheraton, furniture designer and maker, lived at 163 Wardour Street.

Grahame's Seafare

38 Poland Street London W1V 3DA
Tel 071-437 3788 Fax 081-294 1808

Positively New York in its multi-ethnicity, Grahame's is a kosher fish and chip shop owned by a Turk deep in the heart of Soho. Not the obvious place for an intimate or long-drawn-out meal, but an amusing feeding station before a film.

Metro Cinema

11 Rupert Street London W1V 7FS
Tel 071-437 0757

Metro is a surprise – one of the very few modern cinemas in London. Scooped out of a basement and clad in modish *béton brut*, its bar is populated by a noisy and self-regarding community of would-be media lords. For film fanatics it is a haven.

Gerrard Street is the centre of Chinatown. The restaurants are scarcely distinguishable, although each attracts persuasive and argumentative loyalists. Everyone has a good range of *dim sum* and air-dried duck; if you like Chinese food, you can't go wrong picking at random. There are fabulous supermarkets overflowing with Oriental foods and cookware. At night there is a pleasingly sinister atmosphere.

White Tower

1 Percy Street London W1P OET
Tel 071-636 8141 Fax 071-580 1105

Percy Street is what used to be called West Soho, and the White Tower is its oldest established restaurant. Approximately Greek and with a legendary menu carrying painstaking glosses on the true nature of moussaka, the thing about the White Tower is not the cooking (although there is not much wrong with this, provided you have efficient digestion and like Levantine food in the first place), but the environment. The White Tower is fabulously dark and serious, with lots of wood panelling and dark velour. Service is very stately. It is not so much that the White Tower helps you pretend you are in Athens; its emotional effect is less geographically specific and any travelling involved is more to do with time than space. If you would like to pretend that you are in an Anthony Powell novel, taramasalata and imam bayaldi in the White Tower will do the trick nicely. Although not so expensive, **The Little Akropolis 10 Charlotte Street London W1P 1HE Tel 071-636 8198** is a short walk away and provides much the same bang for fewer bucks.

All Saints

7 Margaret Street London W1N 83Q
Tel 071-636 1788

This is the temple of High Anglicanism, the notorious smells and bells. William Butterfield's astonishing design of 1849–59 was described by the architectural critic, Ian Nairn, as an 'orgasm'. The ornament is overwhelming, especially in contrast to the cramped site, set back from an undistinguished street in London's garment district near Oxford Circus.

Leicester Square, an area best avoided unless the noisy mass catering of Chinese canteens on lower Wardour Street amuses you. If, by accident, you find yourself in this hellhole, the French Church is a source of respite. Notre Dame de France, Leicester Place, has elegant doodles by Jean Cocteau, who lied to tell the truth.

Covent Garden and Bloomsbury

The market at Covent Garden was established in the seventeenth century and, like most market areas, it has always had a raffish character, complemented here by a rich literary and theatrical tradition. John Cleland's lascivious *Fanny Hill* lived in Covent Garden and Thomas de Quincey wrote his *Diary of an English Opium Eater* (1822) at 36 Tavistock Street. Johnson actually met Boswell in the house of John Davies, the bookseller, at 8 Russell Street. Since the removal of the fruit markets in the early seventies the area has been through the cycles of gentrification similar to New York's Soho or Paris' Les Halles. To some, the gentrification process has gone too far. The area can be cute, but remains a fabulous draw with some of London's best shops and restaurants. Its dynamism and energy has absorbed the neighbouring and much more staid Bloomsbury, an area dominated by the university, the British Museum and by squares. Once the locale of lawyers, Max Beerbohm noted that "outside their courts lawyers mostly burn with but a dim light". There are serious pursuits in Bloomsbury and a wealth of frivolity, trivial and grave, in Covent Garden.

Wagamama

**Parnell House Streatham Street
London WC1A 1JB
Tel 071-323 9223 Fax 071-323 9224**

Infernal subterranean Sino-Japanese noodle diner in a
bright, noisy, minimalist basement loosely based on an
original design by John Pawson. Interesting, filling, quick
and cheap, waiters take orders on hand-held computers
and transmit by infra-red to teeming, open parallel kitchen.
Mass dining for ambitious school teachers uptown for the
day. Far from intimate, children enjoy the Bladerunner
atmosphere for weekend lunch. Excellent Japanese beer;
sake much more fitting than mediocre house wine.

Joe Allen

**13 Exeter Street London WC2
Tel 071-836 0651 Fax 071-497 2148**

There is actually a man called Joe Allen who runs a pubby
place on 46th Street, New York's restaurant row. For more
than ten years his old friend Richard Polo has been running
the London branch, which achieves a similar character:
busy, noisy, a celebrity favourite, dark, bricks, blackboards,
cheerful, brisk. The menu has evolved from burgers and
steaks, and nods at fashion, but the food, while never less
than good, is only one element in this skilfully managed
exercise in restaurant-as-theatre. The strong sense of
confidence is betrayed by the subtle entrance, which is very
easy to miss. Joe Allen is an institution which might be
brash, but doesn't need to brag. It is London's nearest New
York pub.

Orso

**27 Wellington Street London WC2E 7DA
Tel 071-240 5269 Fax 071-497 2148**

Orso belongs to Joe Allen and is also run by Richard Polo,
who manages this elegantly understated restaurant with
controlled passion and considerable theatrical skill. Orso is
generic 1980s' Italian, one of the very first London
restaurants to reveal the subtleties and sophistication of
Italian regional dishes, while happily managing to avoid their
absurdities; cooking is intelligent and robust, not frivolously
rarefied. The crockery is Tuscan-colourful (from a ceramicist
in Vietri, beloved of Polo's wife, designer Tricia Guild). Orso
may have introduced London to polenta, but resists burnt

rosemary fragments with everything. The menu changes often and there is a good and unusual range of Italian wines. Orso has been a continuous success since the day it opened; restaurant pathologists will study it in decades to come. There is not one single element that is outstanding, but together the food, ambience (vaguely suggestive of Italy in the 1950s, but cooler) and tangible buzz of successful people enjoying themselves make it one of London's finest. Good for late dinner. No credit cards.

After lunch at Orso nothing, not even tea with Lord Clark, could be more agreeable than an hour in the **Courtauld Institute Galleries Somerset House The Strand London WC2R ORN Tel 071-873 2526**. Sir William Chambers' finest building, a replacement for the old Somerset House, was built 1776–80 to house the Royal Academy, Royal Society, Society of Antiquaries and government offices. Appropriately, the Fine Rooms now house one of the world's great collections of Western paintings, developed from the gift of Samuel Courtauld to the University of London. The Fine Rooms still retain traces of the original fabulous decorations by Angelica Kauffmann and Cipriani. The collection is especially rich in Impressionists and Post-Impressionists. Delius once owned Gauguin's melancholic *Nevermore*. Manet's *Bar at the Folies-Bergères* is a glorious liaison between painting and catering.

Christopher's

18 Wellington Street London WC2E 7DD
Tel 071-240 4222 Fax 071-240 3357

Rather as Orso, just opposite, offers Italian food that is difficult to find in Italy, Christopher's offers American food that is hard to find in New York. They airfreight New York strip steak. Possibly modelled on the menu at somewhere 'in' like Manhattan's Gotham Bar and Grill, Christopher's has some interesting deflections of its own. The architectural experience is noteworthy. The building used to be a casino, so you enter, passing the bar on your right, and climb a rather grand staircase. They usually play opera. The interior design is post-modern, but not painfully so. One of the owners is global socialite and gossip journalist Taki Theodoracopoulos; his spiritual presence seems to guarantee a more than average proportion of celebrities. Christopher's is a place people seem to love or hate.

Penhaligon's

41 Wellington Street London WC2E 7BN
Tel 071-836 2150 Fax 071-497 1076

This was the first shop in a small, but remarkable, retail adventure started (and still run by) Sheila Pickles, one-time secretary to Franco Zeffirelli. From the theatre connection Pickles discovered neglected formulae for scents, lotions and unguents by the old perfumier Penhaligon. With backing from Zeffirelli, she created a shop that is an exquisite confection of our, sometimes sentimental, view of the Victorian-Edwardian achievement. Penhaligon's scents for men and women are made of essential oils and are of uncompromising quality. Together with veteran classics such as Hammam and Blenheim, Penhaligon's has introduced new lines, including English Classics. Packaging and presentation are superb.

Boulestin

1A Henrietta Street London WC2E 8PS
Tel 071-836 7061 Fax 071-836 1283

This subterranean restaurant just off Covent Garden's sometimes trashy-flashy piazza owes its name (and ultimately its origins) to F X Boulestin, a professional Frenchman, witty self-publicist and Britain's first television chef. Boulestin is expensive and likes to demonstrate this with interior design and decoration which the aesthetically fastidious will find tiresomely vulgar and affected. It is a temple to a rather dated sort of luxury – perfect if you like obsequious waiters and are impressed by silver cloches, but less appealing to those with an earnest interest in the best of French cooking, however and wherever that may be interpreted.

Library and Museum of the United Grand Lodge of England Freemason's Hall

Great Queen Street London WC2B 5AZ
Tel 071 831 9811 Fax 071-831 6021

A daunting collection of (to some) creepy Masonic regalia; perfect place for reflection during a wet day's walk between the shops of Covent Garden and the more substantial exhibits of the British Museum.

Zwemmer's

72 Charing Cross Road London WC2H OBB
Tel 071-240 1559 Fax 071-836 7049

Very good visual art bookshop.

Poons

27 Lisle Street London WC2H 7BA
Tel 071-437 4549

Not to be confused with Poons of Leicester Square which is
under different management. Notoriously over-rated
Chinatown, but gloomy, menacing authenticity. Everything
wind-dried and damp and metal hotpots.

The Ivy

1 West Street London WC2H 9NE
Tel 071-836 4751 Fax 071-493 9040

The new Ivy is a revival of the old Ivy, a theatreland veteran
with a dubious reputation for questionable food. The new
Ivy is completely different and enjoys the perhaps dubious
distinction of being *absolutely* the favourite restaurant of
London's overpaid and overpopulated advertising
community. The building is splendid, with lots of stained
glass and oak, but the dining room is not especially
comfortable, being rather noisy. Some visitors crick their
necks in the strain to see who else is in. Late at night it can
get I-can't-hear-you loud. Front-of-house service is
impeccable – they seem to know your name as you walk in
the door – but at your table waiter attention can be erratic,
although it is always civil and competent. The menu is a
brilliantly well-conceived and well-executed liaison between
English Classic and Restaurant Modern, so you could order
bruschetta with black pudding, pea soup with rabbit and
polenta. Prices are reasonable. The Ivy is a rare example of
a restaurant of quality open on Sunday. Even rarer is valet
parking.

Now and Zen

4A Upper St Martin's Lane London WC2 9EA
Tel 071-497 0376 Fax 071-437 0641

Now and Zen is the latest in London's most expensive chain
of Chinese restaurants, the first ones to move away from
plastic pagodas, paper lanterns, Cantonese swearing in the
kitchen and flocked dragons, although they still have not
put monosodium glutamate entirely behind them. Chinese

cooking must be the most insensitive and predictable of global cuisines, the distinctions beween cheap and cheerful and dear and dour being less marked than with French or English food. At its worst, Now and Zen seems uncomfortably overpriced, with food not easily distinguishable from what is available at one fifth of the price elsewhere. At its best it can be interesting, and there are curiosities on the menu worth testing. But the St Martin's Lane branch is especially noteworthy for its imaginative, cool, clever architecture by the American Rick Mather, who has made Now and Zen into a coruscating, glass, air and water California-style oriental food temple. There is a ground-floor sushi bar.

Mon Plaisir

21 Monmouth Street London WC2H 9DD
Tel 071-836 7243 Fax 071-379 0121

Alain Lhermitte's Mon Plaisir, in one of Covent Garden's more interesting (ie less spoilt) streets, is a deep and passionate interpretation of the idea of France which so beguiles the English: garlic, crusty bread, saucy waiters, flavoursome food, quaffable wine and unfrightening prices. Interestingly, this is the very same version of 'France' that the French are trying to put behind them. The food is never less than good, although since Mon Plaisir was extended four or five years ago, it can become disagreeably noisy and sweaty in the evening. Still, at lunchtime a bottle of Fleurie, onion soup, entrecôte/frites and Boulette d'Avesnes is a punctuation in shopping that is very hard to beat.

Monmouth Coffee Company

27 Monmouth Street London WC2H 9DD
Tel 071-379 4337 Fax 071-240 2442

A very good supplier of coffee and coffee accessories.

The Tea House

5 Neal Street London WC2H 9PU
Tel 071-240 7539 Fax 071-836 8395

Just around the corner from the Monmouth Coffee Company, the Tea House caters to tea enthusiasts.

The **Neal Street** area has a strip of small shops, best appreciated serially. **Freud Limited 198 Shaftesbury Avenue London WC2H 8JL Tel 071-831 1071** is a

1980s' curiosity, a bizarre retail mix of bar and household accessories. **The Astrology Shop 78 Neal Street London WC2H 9PA Tel 071-497 1001 Fax 071-497 0344** offers customized horoscopes. **The Hat Shop 58 Neal Street London WC2H 9PA Tel 071-836 6718 Fax 071-240 3634** is an interesting milliners – pointless to look here for the everyday. **Ray Man 64 Neal Street London WC2H 9PA Tel 071-240 1776** sells eastern musical instruments. **The Kite Store 48 Neal Street London WC2H 9PA Tel 071-836 1666 Fax 071-836 2510** is a specialist kite shop with a range from £5.95 (for the Quicksilver Mylar Octopus) to £420 (for the Rare Air Force 10 Graphite).

Neal Street Restaurant

26 Neal Street London WC2H 9PS
Tel 071-836 8368/071-497 1361
Fax 071-497 1361

Neal Street is a landmark restaurant, at least in terms of London folklore and in the history of modern interior design. What is now the restaurant was the space left over when Terence Conran's original design studios moved into an old banana warehouse in 1970, marking the symbolic origins of the regeneration of the area. With partners, designer Oliver Gregory and art dealer John Kasmin, Conran created a restaurant that is a monument to 1970s style: generous details, tiles, Bauhaus chairs, spotlights, good napery, good tableware and lots of good, contemporary art. A sort of Habitat *de luxe*. Food has never been anything *terribly* special, but since Conran's brother-in-law, television celebrity and mushroom fanatic Antonio Carluccio, bought the place, interesting funghi appear on the sedate menu in season. The wine list, like the restaurant, is astonishingly expensive and not very imaginative, although the service is usually very, very professional and assured. Downstairs is an attractive, but neglected, cocktail bar, one of London's nicest modern rooms. The Neal Street Restaurant is an institution spoiling itself with a combination of opportunistic pricing and cooking that is no better than good enough, but, nevertheless, a visit is still an exceptional experience, even for the rich.

Carluccio's

28A Neal Street London WC2H 9PS

Tel 071-240 1487 Fax 071-497 1361

Next door to the Neal Street Restaurant, of which he is
proprietor, Antonio Carluccio has opened an exclusive,
interesting and cruelly expensive food shop. It carries a small,
but very interesting range of expensive Italian curiosities. Idle
purchases are not for the faint-hearted or short-in-pocket.

Smith's

33 Shelton Street London WC2H 9HT

Tel 071-379 0310

Christina Smith is a living Covent Garden legend, landlord
to many, and provider of interesting businesses, including
the curious **Neal Street East 5 Neal Street London
WC2H 9PU Tel 071-240 0135**, an emporium of
oriental bric-à-brac. Smith's is a hybrid gallery-restaurant,
with the eating and drinking in the vast basement. It is an
agreeable curiosity to visit, especially if you are in a large
party, but the quality of the food and catering is erratic.

David Newell

55 Shelton Street London WC2H 9EE

Tel 071-836 1000

Restoration of clocks, watches, musical boxes, barometers
and automata.

Neal's Yard Dairy

17 Shorts Gardens London WC2H 9AT

Tel 071-379 7646 Fax 071-240 2442

Neal's Yard Dairy sells a complete range of familiar and rare
British cheeses; assistants are knowledgeable and helpful.

Neal's Yard Wholefoods Ltd

21-23 Shorts Gardens London WC2H 9AS

Tel 071-379 8553 Fax 071-240 6095

Now almost fully evolved from the clogs and kaftan era,
Neal's Yard Wholefoods carries huge and interesting stocks
of beans, pulses and dried fruits.

Windle

41 Shorts Gardens London WC2H 9AP

Tel 071-497 2393

A very thorough hairdressing service.

Edward Stanford

12-14 Long Acre London WC2E 9LP
Tel 071-836 1321 Fax 071-836 0189

Established in 1852 and recently refurbished, Stanford's is the largest map shop in the world, with a huge range of survey and touring maps, maritime and aeronautical charts, as well as globes and books.

Paul Smith

41-44 Floral Street London WC2E 9DJ
Tel 071-836 7828 Fax 071-379 0241

If one shop characterizes the urban renewal of Covent Garden, it is Paul Smith. Now Britain's most successful menswear designer, the laid back but ambitious Smith opened a small, purpose-built shop in rundown Floral Street in 1978. Then and now the Smith style is English classic, with an emphasis on quality and traditional cloths, but taken out of the ordinary by clever twists and quirks sufficient to serve notice that wearers have not sold out to middle age, while simultaneously projecting attractive career-serving notions about senses of quality, respect for tradition and understated style. Paul Smith clothes are aimed directly at the too old to rock, too young to die generation. The original concrete shop has now greatly expanded to include premises next door, fitted out with wood panelling from an old chocolate factory. Old Paul Smith hands say they notice an occasionally desperate lunge at novelty nowadays; the shop now also carries accessories as well as clothes, but these you can ignore. There is still nowhere better to buy a tie or a shirt.

The Sanctuary

12 Floral Street London WC2E 9DH
Tel 071-240 9635

A luxurious and very well-equipped women's fitness, health and therapy centre.

Clarins Health Centre

Garden Pharmacy 119 Long Acre London WC2E
9PA Tel 071-379 1225 Fax 071-379 5194

A near neighbour and close rival to the Sanctuary.

Jones

13 Floral Street London WC2E 9DH
Tel 071-240 8312 Fax 071-240 8310

For those still interested, avant-garde menswear.

Bertram Rota

9-11 Langley Court London WC2E 9JY
Tel 071-836 0723 Fax 071-497 9058

A very superior and handsome antiquarian bookshop

Outlaws' Club

49 Endell Street London WC2H 9AJ
Tel 071-379 6940

This is the reincarnation of Covent Garden jeweller Detail. Then as now Angela McLoughin sells wonderfully absurd and often rather clever jewellery.

St Paul's

Bedford Street London WC2E 9ED
Tel 071-836 5221

This church by Inigo Jones, known as 'the handsomest barn in England', was designed as the central feature of the Covent Garden piazza. The present building is a replica of the original of 1631–38 which burnt down in a 1795 fire. The replica may have lost authenticity, but a great deal of the poetry remains. Its majestic, masculine starkness denies some of the delicacy and exquisiteness of Inigo Jones's original, but it is a compelling monument none the less.

Rules

35 Maiden Lane London WC2E 7LB
Tel 071-836 2559

London's oldest restaurant in continuous existence, now too well known by foreign travel editors and their readers to be taken entirely seriously, although if you are in the mood for intense nostalgia, the period decor can be comforting. In season, game is excellent. Good wine list.

Savoy Grill and River Restaurant

The Strand London WC2R 0EU
Tel 071-836 4343 Fax 071-240 6040

This is the scriptural home of the great hotelier Cesar Ritz and the great chef, Auguste Escoffier. Between them they made dining out a middle-class entertainment and to one contemporary The Savoy of the 1880s turned London into "a place worth living in". The two modern restaurants have different entrances and separate chefs. The Grill (patronised by intimidatingly important industrialists, padded politicians and media lords who may order the famous 'Omelette Arnold Bennett') is on the left. The more human River Restaurant overlooks Thames and is a good choice for an impressive breakfast, if you *need* an impressive breakfast. The American Bar is a classic cocktail hour institution.

A walk around the back of the Savoy leads to the area known as the Adelphi, site of the original Adelphi Terrace built by the Adam brothers between 1768 and 1774. Here is the densest collection of theatrical ghosts: John Galsworthy and James Barrie lived in Robert Adam's old house at 1-3 Robert Street; famous residents of the terrace itself included David Garrick, Richard D'Oyly Carte, Thomas Hardy and George Bernard Shaw. Not far away Samuel Pepys lived at 12 and 14 Buckingham Street from 1679 to 1688.

Museum Street, just opposite the British Museum, has one restaurant; **Museum Street Café 47 Museum Street London WC1 1LY Tel 071-405 3211**, which is a gastronomic Guide camp with an atmosphere of toiling pleasure and sanctity. Real breads baked on premises, very limited choice. Good ingredients, highly competent execution, but sullen, amateurish feel. Take your own wine. Around the corner in Coptic Street is a branch of the Pizza Express chain in a jolly converted dairy. Probably a better bet for lunch.

But Museum Street is famous for its booksellers. The better ones are: **Ulysses 31 & 40 Museum Street London WC1A 1LH Tel 071-637 5862 Fax 071-831 1600** modern first editions; **The Print Room 37 Museum Street London WC1A 1LP Tel 071-430 0159 Fax 071-831 9150** general antiquarian books and prints; **The Wellspring Bookshop 40A Museum Street London WC1A 1LT Tel 071-831 1997** a Rudolf Steiner specialist; **Vanbrugh Rare Books 40A Museum Street London WC1A 1LT Tel 071-404 0733 Fax 071-404 1262; Cartoon Gallery 44 Museum Street London WC1 1LX Tel 071-242 5335**.

Abbot & Holder

30 Museum Street London WC1A 1LH
Tel 071-637 3981

An old-established picture dealer with an admirable
tradition of selling paintings and prints at affordable prices
'that can be bought from income'.

S J Shrubshole

43 Museum Street London WC1A 1LY
Tel 071-405 2712

Old English silver.

James Smith & Sons

53 New Oxford Street London WC1A 1BQ
Tel 071-836 4731

Smith is a perfect treasure, a wonderfully eccentric shop
devoted to absolutely nothing but umbrellas and walking
sticks. It is rare, even humbling, to visit something
absolutely unique: there is nothing like James Smith
anywhere else on earth.

Jessop's

67 Russell Street London WC1B 3BN
Tel 071-831 3640 Fax 071-831 3956

Britain's leading antique camera shop, with an excellent
range of all formats always available. Very knowledgeable
staff can discriminate finely between all species of Canon,
Nikon, Leica, Gandolfi and others. A terrific place for
technophiles to browse.

Bloomsbury gave its name to a tiresome set of ego
tormentors and projectors, including John Maynard Keynes,
who lived at 46 Gordon Square, and Lytton Strachey, who
lived a few houses away at 51. But there are other ghosts as
well: poetess Christina Rossetti lived and died at 30
Torrington Square, and her brother, the painter and poet
Dante Gabriel Rossetti, lived in 1851 at 17 Red Lion Square,
where he was succeeded as a resident by William Morris and
Sir Edward Burne-Jones.

Renoir Cinema

Brunswick Square London WC1
Tel 071-837 8402

The Renoir is the Bloomsbury branch of a small chain

(including The Lumiere in St Martin's Lane and The Chelsea in King's Road) of well-managed modern cinemas showing quality continental films.

Petrie Museum of Egyptian Archaeology

University College Gower St. London WC1E 6BT
Tel 071-387 7050 ext 2884

Ancient Egyptian antiquities from the trawls of W M Flinders Petrie.

Percival David Foundation of Chinese Art

53 Gordon Square London WC1H OPD
Tel 071-387 3909

A gift to the University of London by Sir Percival David in 1950, a reference collection of Chinese ceramics, augmented by the Mountstuart W Elphinstone Collection. A world-class range of Chinese ceramics from the ninth to the nineteenth century, but especially strong on eighteenth-century court taste. On three floors of what was once a private house, domestic scale and profound objects instil a Zen-like state of calm. You leave in a reflective mood.

Sir John Soane's Museum

13 Lincoln's Inn Fields London WC2A 3BP
Tel 071-405 2107

This extraordinary place, one of the most curious museums in the world, was the great architect's home for the last twenty-four years of his life (1813–47). It is a building of exceptional architectural quality, housing a spell-binding collection of antiquities which bridge the gulf between occult arcana and scholarly evidence of past civilizations. It is picturesque and classical at the same time, rich evidence of a life of idiosyncratic genius balanced halfway between the old cabinet of curiosities of the *dilettanti* and the eclecticism of the decorator. Although there are exceptional exhibits – Hogarth's *The Rake's Progress* and the sarcophagus of Set I, for instance – the essential magical quality of Soane's Museum is a sense of personality. There are few buildings anywhere with such a profound sense of place. Soane's architecture was inspired by 'hazard and surprise'. Here you find them mixed with invention: the marvellous Monk's Parlour was added in 1824 for the fantastical Padre Giovanni.

Dickens' House Museum

48 Doughty Street London WC1N 2LF
Tel 071-405 2127

Dickens's home for only three years (1837–39), but one of
great productivity. Here he wrote *Pickwick Papers*, *Nicholas
Nickleby* and most of *Oliver Twist*. This cluttered shrine
brings together Dickensiana from all his life, including the
clerk's desk from his legal apprenticeship at Gray's Inn (in
the morning room). The drawing room is especially
authentic.

Jewish Museum

Woburn House Tavistock Square London
WC1H OEP Tel 071-388 4525

A cramped and crowded museum, especially illustrative of
Jewish life in Britain before the large Ashkenazim
immigration of the late nineteenth century. For instance, a
Staffordshire mug shows the fight between Daniel Mendoza
and Richard Humphreys in 1788 – an important event in the
history of boxing. There is a marvellously gloomy Dutch
'vanitas' painting of 1681 by Benjamin Senior Godines.
Inscriptions in Hebrew and Spanish about the futility and
frailty of earthly ambitions.

National Gallery

Trafalgar Square WC2N 5BN
Tel 071-839 3321

One of the world's greatest picture galleries, evolving from
the private collection of the financier John Julius Angerstein.
Of the National Gallery Logan Pearsall Smith said, 'How
often my soul visits...and how seldom I go there myself.'
Originally in his Pall Mall house, it moved to Sir William
Wilkins's new 'National' gallery in 1838. The Sainsbury wing,
designed by Robert Venturi, was added in 1990. If you were
familiar with the National Gallery, you would have an
exceptionally thorough knowledge of the history of art. The
gallery can claim to have a major work by every significant
artist, although perhaps the outstanding works are Jan Van
Eyck's *Arnolfini Marriage* (1434), the epitome of northern
renaissance portraiture, an exquisite, quiet painting, dense
with technique and symbolism; Piero della Francesca's *The
Baptism of Christ* (early 1450s), a painting of monumental
calm suffused with mathematical spirit; Leonardo da Vinci's
mysterious *Virgin and Child with Saint John the Baptist and*

Saint Anne (c 1508), a beautiful, but complex and controversial, cartoon which perplexed Sigmund Freud; Hans Holbein's *The Ambassadors* (1533), a wonderful account of worldly fame and the transience of earthly success – the broken string on the lute and the anamorphosis of the distorted skull in the foreground are both suggestive of death; Titian's *Bacchus and Ariadne* (1523), the brilliant Venetian colourist's glorious celebration of paganism; Johannes Vermeer's *A Young Woman Standing at a Virginal* (c 1670) is a masterpiece of genre painting, but also a brilliant essay in the effects of light; John Constable's *Hay Wain* (1821) is perhaps the greatest English oil painting, certainly the one which best summarizes the national preoccupation with the countryside and weather. Here more than ever it looks as though it is about to rain.

National Portrait Gallery

St Martin's Place London WC2H OHE
Tel 071-930 1552

Next door to the National Gallery, this collection is apparently less spectacular, but more likely to afford the visitor the luxury of quiet contemplation. Besides, there *are* marvellous paintings. It is an intensely strange and moving experience to sit before the sole portrait of Shakespeare done from the life, or see Joshua Reynolds's self-portrait. The gallery opened in 1859, after a parliamentary debate in which Lord Palmerston explained the moral and educational basis for creating a national Valhalla. Impressive labelling summarizes achievements of the sitters. Very good shop.

Knightsbridge and Belgravia

Knightsbridge and Belgravia are *the* smartest part of London.
Knightsbridge presents the last refinements of international
shopping *de luxe* with coruscating famous-name international
boutiques and sedate, but absorbing, commercial institutions:
Harrods and Harvey Nichols. Belgravia is the adjacent
residential area, housing *de luxe*, magnificent in scale and
its homogenized grandeur. Built by Thomas Cubitt for the Duke
of Westminster, it takes its name from the Grosvenor family
village of Belgrave in Leicestershire. The Duke of Westminster,
the wealthiest individual in Britain, still owns much of the
area. It is said he can travel from London to Bristol without
leaving his own property.

The 5th Floor at Harvey Nichols

Knightsbridge London SW1
Tel 071-235 5250 Fax 071-235 5020

A revelation by the standards of department store restaurants *anywhere*, an apocalyptic occurrence in the context of London. The top floor of the capital's grandest store has been turned over to food. The Food Market is an impoverished Dean & De Luca, pleasant and interesting, but let down by so-so merchandise. The restaurant and bar have been designed by Julyan Wickham, one of the smartest restaurant architects of the past decade or so. Armchairs are absurdly tricksy, but open plan is bright, civilized, agreeable. Service is smooth, pleasant, confident. Food is superb, among the very best in London. Chef Henry Harris was Simon Hopkinson's number two at Bibendum. He has inherited the style (robust Anglo-French) *and* the competence. The 5th Floor is at least as good, less intimidating and less expensive. One of the very best places for lunch, a mite characterless by night.

Micheline Arcier

7 William Street London SW1X 9HL
Tel 071-235 3545

An old-fashioned but very professional and highly regarded aromatherapist.

Caffe Monpelliano

144 Brompton Road London SW3 1HY
Tel 071-225 2926

A bright, smart, ground-floor, fast, all-day-service café-restaurant in a grand but humourless stretch of Knightsbridge. Superficially, there is nothing about Caffe Monpelliano (an offspring of a rather fussy, posturing, old-established Knightsbridge Italian around the corner) to account for its phenomenal success, although the coffee and middleweight Italian food are moderately priced and well executed, but Monpelliano is full all day. In the morning young Italian couples in cashmere smoke cigarettes with their coffee and jaw for hours. At lunchtime a busier working crowd takes over. In the afternoon it is a great place to read a newspaper, and in the evening there is another altogether more relaxed ambience.

Caroline Charles

56 Beauchamp Place London SW3 1NQ
Tel 071-225 3197 Fax 071-584 2521

Caroline Charles is one of the very, very few 1960s'
survivors with sense, integrity and reputation intact.
Recently she has evolved from conservative and elegant
couture for mature women of all ages (including the
Princess of Wales) into larger premises selling men's and
women's ready-to-wear clothes and accessories. The
premises are unusually large and handsome for
Beauchamp Place.

Margaret Howell

29 Beauchamp Place London SW3 1NJ
Tel 071-584 2462 Fax 071-584 6925

Margaret Howell is either above fashion or left behind by it –
no one can ever be absolutely certain. She does well-made,
conservative, generously cut clothes for men and women,
using fine, traditional materials.

Bill Bentley's

31 Beauchamp Place London SW3 INU
Tel 071-589 5080

There is nothing particularly special about Bill Bentley's,
except that it is rather a pleasant place to be – a dark,
woodlined wine bar with a small garden for summer
drinking, where people enjoy meeting, especially early
evening. Soigné staff and customers, decent wine. Cooked
dishes unremarkable; eat smoked salmon sandwiches or
oysters.

San Lorenzo

22 Beauchamp Place London SW3 1NH
Tel 071-584 1074

The cooking in San Lorenzo is fine, although its reference
points are the imaginary dishes of Italian restaurants
established in the days before you could buy ciabatta in a
kosher supermarket. The wine list is rather negligent of the
interesting new-wave Italian wines, but these are beside the
point. You enter San Lorenzo from Beauchamp Place, a
street which doesn't quite know if it is rag-trade floozie or
Knightsbridge-chic, with its odd mixture of exclusive
couturiers and bargain stores. In fact, it is a bit of both.
Inside, it is quite an appealing architectural experience,

one of those rare establishments that appears more
complicated than it actually is: dark corners, mirrors and a
conservatory (with a sliding roof for sunny days). There are
no credit cards and service can be abrupt if they don't know
you; staff are concentrating on the regulars, but since these
(quite genuinely) include Eric Clapton and the Princess of
Wales, no one seems to mind.

Luba's Bistro

6 Yeoman's Row London SW3 2AH
Tel 071-589 2950

Luba's is on the borders of Knightsbridge-Kensington and
is an institution, like Lubyanka is an institution. Famous for
its screamingly awful interior of coloured discharge tubes
and plastic table-cloths, this cheap restaurant was a
favourite with impoverished staff of the V&A and penny-
pinching researchers using the National Art Library. The
cooking is a debased, proletarianized version of hard to
digest East European generalities, with lots of emphasis on
fat and an insouciance about subtleties of taste and texture.
Dishes can be overdone or underdone and are never quite
right. Since after lunch at Luba's you may feel you will never
eat again, it is a must for the chronically greedy. Take your
own wine (there is a branch of the excellent Oddbins chain
at the top of the road). Always an event, although not
always a very pleasurable one.

It is impossible to know what to say about **Harrods
Knightsbridge London SW1 Tel 071-730 1234**,
as difficult to summarize as the British Museum. It is vast,
crowded, has surly staff and is increasingly remote in most
departments (although there are some exceptions) from
traditional ideas about service and courtesy. And yet,
despite all the changes, Harrods still carries an
astonishingly complete stock of worthwhile merchandise. It
has an excellent book department and a genuinely
knowledgeable watch repairer. Much of the rest is on the
decline or ascent, depending on your point of view, towards
tinselly international glamour. The Food Hall is still full of
marvellous things, but completely ruined by crocodiles of
tourists taking photographs of arrangements of wet fish.

Cutler & Gross

16 Knightsbridge Green London SW1X 7QL
Tel 071-581 2250

Tony Gross is the best ophthalmologist or, at least, the best designer of glasses in London. He always stocks *the* most interesting frames, which are made for him by a network of craftsmen. Gross's designs, which span the gulf between retro and techno, are often inspired by cuttings from old and new magazines. You can get of-the-moment frames inspired either by George Bush at Kennebunkport (1992) or Audrey Hepburn in Chamonix (1955).

Capital Hotel

Basil Street London SW3 1AT
Tel 071-589 5171 Fax 071-225 0011

On the face of it unpromising, a banal modern building with a fluffy (Nina Campbell) decorator's interior in *faux* Louis something. But things get better when you experience the service. The general air of professionalism is superb and serene, and the dining room restful and aloof from the backstreet shoppers' bustle (if you can ignore the awful swags, drapes and silly neo-classical chairs). The lunch menus are extremely good value and immaculately executed, with good ingredients and sharp definition of flavours. More fun than shopping, this is one of those *very* rare restaurants where an air of benign relaxation overwhelms you after a meal.

Basil Street Hotel

Basil Street London SW3 1AH
Tel 071-581 3311 Fax 071-581 3693

A comfortable time-warp experience for tea or breakfast close to Harrods.

Chelsea, Fulham and Battersea

Chelsea has always been London's artists' headquarters, with bohemian traditions fastidiously maintained by members of The Chelsea Arts Club. Nowadays the non-descript Fulham has acquired some of its romantic lustre. Even transpontine Battersea is – not entirely ironically – known as 'south Chelsea'. Sir Thomas More's Beaufort House was here, as was Henry VIII's farm, but nineteenth century development and the Luftwaffe eradicated most of the ancient village. The area contains the beginning and the end of nineteenth century church-building. In Sydney Street is one of the very first Gothic Revival churches, St Luke's by James Savage (1820-1824). In Sloane Street is J.D. Sedding's Holy Trinity, the perfect Arts and Crafts church with windows by Burne-Jones (1888-1890). King's Road was originally the private royal route to the palace at Hampton Court. Its source in Sloane Square is the epicentre of fashionable London, a square with a curiously continental feel, although continuously isolated by traffic. In 1956 John Osborne's epochal "Look Back in Anger" was first performed at the Royal Court Theatre. The irreverence was maintained throughout the sixties when the King's Road was the pendulum of Swinging London.

Simply Nico

48A Rochester Row London SW1P 1JU
Tel 071-630 8061

Simply Nico is sited in that area of Victoria between the ecclesiastical hinterland of the cathedrals and the hellish housing estates of Pimlico. The proprietor is a famously truculent and rebarbative chef, as well known for his tantrums as his cooking, neither of which are always pleasing. Simply Nico is a cut-price, or at least *prix fixe*, formula restaurant, a spin-off from his more magnificent establishments (now losing some of their lustre). You will not be pampered, but the food can be good. It is in a pleasant backwater close to nowhere in particular, which makes it fine for certain sorts of lunches.

Green's

Marsham Street London SW1P 4LA
Tel 071-834 9552 Fax 071-233 6047

Green's is special in a very specific sense: it is close to the Houses of Parliament and its food and ambience replicate clubby notions of Olde England, which also serve to make it attractive to MPs. Lots of fake genteel panelling, 1980s' leather banquettes, bulk-buy sporting prints and nursery puddings. A great place for voyeurs.

Mijanou

143 Ebury Street London SW1W 9QN
Tel 071-730 4099

Going to Mijanou is, one imagines, like going to a very old-fashioned and fairly exclusive brothel. It is in that part of London where embassy-Belgravia fringes Victoria Coach Station, an area full of rooming hotels and fly-by-nights. You have to ring a bell to gain access. Atmosphere is very much that of a club *privée*. Inside, behind the nets, it is intimate, not to say cramped. Cooking is fairly complicated French, and often satisfyingly complete. There is an eclectic wine list, organized with an embarrassing numerical coding which tells you in a rather schoolmasterly way what wine goes well with what dish. Mijanou is a happily eccentric restaurant and an excellent choice for a discreet lunch or dinner. There is no celebrity hum, but you get comforting food of quality in agreeable surroundings. Upper-middle prices.

Peter Jones

Sloane Square London SW1W 8EE
Tel 071-730 3434 Fax 071-730 9645

Peter Jones *the shop* is a Chelsea institution; apparently a humdrum department store, it supplies Chelsea matrons and their mates with absolutely every personal and domestic requisite for lives split between town houses and the shires, and plays an almost mystical, religiously supportive role in their lives. Visiting social anthropologists will be amazed. It is noteworthy that there is no food hall – people shop at Partridge's just around the corner in Sloane Street. Peter Jones *the building* is one of London's most interesting Modern Movement buildings. Designed by Sir Charles Reilly in 1936, its magnificent glass façade – inspired somewhat by Eric Mendelssohn – takes-up the curve of King's Road, thus managing to be both picturesque and modernist at the same time.

Sloane Health Shop

32 Sloane Square London SW1W 8AQ
Tel 071-823 6323 Fax 071-823 5521

The façade is unpromising – no more attractive than any provincial chemist – but the Sloane Health Shop stocks a vast range of specialist products.

David Mellor

4 Sloane Square London SW1W 8EE
Tel 071-730 4259

The shop owned by Britain's outstanding cutlery designer. Range of merchandise (which is intended to appeal to the serious cook, although Chelsea wedding lists are a custom here) is limited only by the exercise of Mellor's own taste, which is purist and absolutely dedicated to quality.

Patrick Cox

8 Symons Street London SW3 2TJ
Tel 071-730 6504 Fax 071-730 1722

Patrick Cox makes men's and women's shoes whose oddness sometimes closes the gap between astonishing and perverse. Interesting decor.

John Sandoe (Books) Ltd

10 Blacklands Terrace London SW3 TSR

Tel 071-589 9473 Fax 071-581 2084

An apparently chaotic, but in fact very well-stocked, independent bookshop with knowledgeable staff.

Jon Bannenberg

6 Burnsall Street London SW3 3ST

Tel 071-352 4851 Fax 071-352 8444

By appointment only, but well worth any necessary deception. From his very attractive Chelsea studios Jon Bannenberg, an amiable, sun-tanned, opera-loving Australian, designs spectacular yachts for the very, very rich.

Antiquarius

131 King's Road London SW3

Tel 071-351 5353

Antiquarius is a huge covered market of antique stalls halfway along King's Road, convenient for the crowded Chelsea Potter pub. Many of the stallholders have the patina of debauchery that made Chelsea such a celebrated 1960s' locale. A dismaying number of stalls sell expensive rubbish, but some pockets of excellence remain. Jasmine Cameron sells fabulous period fountain pens, drawing instruments and colouring boxes from a minute stall. Chelsea Clocks and Antiques specializes in timepieces. Antiquarius has a café, but it is best avoided. Use the Chelsea Potter pub or the nearby Picasso coffee bar, a not specially distinguished, but somehow specially favoured Chelsea haunt.

Chenil Galleries

181 King's Road London SW3

Tel 071-351 5353

About 500 metres west of Antiquarius is the smaller, rather more exclusive Chenil Galleries, where there are some other outstanding specialist dealers, including Steinberg and Tolkien, who sell 1930s' costume jewellery.

Anouska Hempel

2 Pond Place London SW3

Tel 071-589 4191 Fax 071-584 1800

Lady Weinberg, proprietor of Blake's Hotel (p.74), is also a couturier.

L'Odéon

173 Fulham Road London SW3 6JW
Tel 071-581 3640

A dealer in late nineteenth-century and early twentieth-century applied arts.

Lewis M Kaplan

50 Fulham Road London SW3 6HH
Tel 071-589 3108 Fax 071-584 6328

A dignified and relaxed gallery specializing in 1920s' and 1930s' decorative arts, run by the fastidious and ironic Gordon Watson. Expensive, but special – the ideal place to buy vintage Cartier jewellery.

David Gill Gallery

60 Fulham Road London SW3 6HH
Tel 071-589 5946 Fax 071-584 9184

A small and stylish new gallery specializing in interesting applied arts.

Souleiado

171 Fulham Road London SW3 6JW
Tel 071-589 6180 Fax 071-823 9252

The London outlet of Charles Demery's charming Provençal fabric business. Souleiado's style is floral and colourful. For more severe fabrics go to **Timney Fowler Ltd 388 King's Road London SW3 5UZ Tel 071-351 6562 Fax 071-352 0351**.

Johnny Moke

396 King's Road London SW10
Tel 071-351 2232

Like so much else in the World's End part of Chelsea, Johnny Moke is an institution. This eccentrically talented shoe designer sells quirky men's and women's shoes, and makes to order.

The Argyll

316 King's Road London SW3 5UH
Tel 071-352 0025 Fax 071-352 1652

The Argyll is in a stretch of King's Road which in some lights appears to be entirely restaurants, few of any real quality, although some of charm (including the antique Thierry's and the hip Ed's Easy Diner). The Argyll raises the quality of the game. It is run by the same team that created the recession-hit Sutherlands in the West End, a restaurant that became a *succès d'estime*, but the Argyll has yet to achieve a *succès de curiosité*. The design is striking, very austere and white from the road, spare and white inside, but with interesting, old-fashioned dining chairs. It is spacious and comfortable, with an easy atmosphere. The cooking is modern and efficient, but not in any way exceptional. The Argyll is a serious restaurant, but has not yet defined a unique identity.

Green & Stone

259 King's Road London SW3 5EL
Tel 071-352 6521 Fax 071-351 1098
Excellent artists' suppliers with interesting stock, including fine papers and Sennelier pastels.

Vivian's

360 King's Road SW10
Tel 071-351 3180
A very superior, very expensive, very brightly lit, but rewarding delicatessen.

Furniture Cave

533 King's Road London W10 OTZ
Tel 071-352 4229
The Furniture Cave is a vast collection of antique dealers housed in a huge but undistinguished building in the no man's land between King's Road and New King's Road. It sets the style for the collection of Lots Road auction houses, especially **Bonham's** and the **Lots Road Galleries 71 Lots Road London SW10 ORN Tel 071-351 7771 Fax 071-376 8349**, where occasionally junk can be mistaken for antique. Most of the stuff on display in the various dealers is under-nourished, over-polished, over-priced and depressingly ugly, of interest only to those with an obsessive concern to acquire the old rather than the good. To misquote Ruskin, the Furniture Cave is full of 'fatal oldness', but it is still possible to make chance finds of quality. Here Anthony Outred specializes in magnificent garden monuments, but his prices are very high.

Chelsea Beach

116 Lots Road London SW10 ORT
Tel 071-352 7771

Just opposite the Bonham's auction rooms in Lots Road and next door to the appealing Ferret and Firkin pub is a genuinely strange shop called Chelsea Beach run by a genuinely strange man called Hans Muller. He makes curious women's wear in a style which defies succinct characterization, but consistently manages to be assertive when it is not downright ugly. Of great interest to eccentrics and amateurs of the bizarre, although one sometimes suspects his entire market might be exclusively transvestite.

Harvey's Canteen

Harbour Yard Chelsea Harbour
London SW10 OXD
Tel 071-351 7330 Fax 071-351 6189

Harvey's Canteen, where the actor Michael Caine is co-proprietor, is the diffusion of Marco Pierre White's celebrated and very expensive Harvey's restaurant. There are a number of bad things about it. First, it is in Chelsea Harbour, one of the most hideous and hateful of modern residential developments, at once sentimental and harsh, staffed by surly Cockney Volkspolizei, who do a very good job of maintaining a general air of malevolence. Second, its decor is appallingly ugly and conceited, with the worst lighting and layout I have ever seen in a restaurant. Third, the service is joylessly anarchic. The food, however, is on the cusp of excellence and, despite the awfulness of the place, people keep on going back. There is no surer sign of a good restaurant.

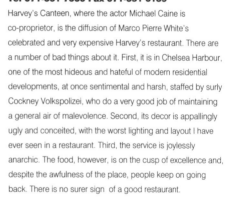

New King's Road is a linear cornucopia of antique shops, mostly of very good quality; examples include **Trowbridge Gallery 555 King's Road London SW6 2EB Tel 071-371 8733 Fax 071-371 8138** specializing in supplying the interior design trade with prints mounted in astonishingly elaborate frames using more than eighty different techniques; **Alastair Brown 560 King's Road London SW6 2DZ Tel 071-736 8077 Fax 071-736 3625**; **Shield & Allen 584-586 King's Road London SW6 2DX Tel 071-736 7145 Fax 071-736 2009** often has spectacular pieces; **Ferenc Toth 598A King's Road London SW6 2DX Tel 071-731 2063** specializing in mirrors.

The centre of gravity of the New King's Road antique belt is held by **Christopher Wray 600 King's Road London SW6 2DX Tel 071-736 8434 Fax 071-731 3507**. The word emporium is often misused, except in this case. Christopher Wray is a vast storehouse of lighting, mostly in embarrassingly poor taste – someone in the organization still thinks there is a Victorian revival going on – but impressive in its size, scale and conviction.

David Linley Company

1 New King's Road London SW6 4SB Tel 071-736 6886 Fax 071-736 9686

Here, in a modish reversal of social Darwinism, the Queen's nephew has become a cabinet-maker, next door to London's leading Harley-Davidson distributor. Linley has a characteristic modern classical style, often using contrasting inlays or Venetian *trompe l'oeil*.

Hackett Ltd

65B New King's Road London SW6 4SG Tel 071-371 7964 Fax 071-498 3533

It is hard to say whether Hackett led or followed the young-fogey phenomenon, but the fit between cause and effect is perfect. Middle-priced men's clothes of a trenchant conservatism, the sartorial parallel to the revival of lush country house interior decorating in the 1980s.

Beyond the upper middle-class *brocante* of New King's Road is **Parson's Green**, a comfortable area where the tension of the big city is noticeably diffused by the approach of suburbia. Parson's Green has a few pleasant shops, including **Patrizia Wigan 72 New King's Road London SW6 4LT Tel 071-736 3336** for custom children's wear, and **Aimi 56 New King's Road London SW6 Tel 071-371 5353 Fax 071-371 0040** for lingerie. Up a sinister, light-industrial lane you can find **Fullbore Motors Heathman's Yard Heathman's Road London SW6 4TJ Tel 071-371 5931**, where a roguish young team imports the atrocious Hindustan Ambassador, a reincarnation of a mid-1950s' Morris Oxford, from Bombay.

On Pimlico Road, Pimlico Green, and at the bottom of Holbein Place there is another rich cluster of antique shops.

Sotheran 80 Pimlico Road London SW1W 8PI Tel 071-730 8756 Fax 071-823 6090 specializes in fine antique prints and drawings, tending to concentrate on architecture, archaeology, gardening, zoology and botany, but there are bargains to be had; prices begin as low as £25. The anchor of the area is **Bennison 91 Pimlico Road London SW1W 8PH Tel 071-730 1516**, although past its best since the death of the proprietor; **Westenholz 76-78 Pimlico Road London SW1W 8LS Tel 071-824 8090 Fax 071-823 5913** frequently has massive furniture of spare line and very singular quality – no frou-frou here. Piers von Westenholz is an elegant celebrity among the foppish antique trade. **Richard Miles 8 Holbein Place London SW1W 8NI Tel 071-730 1957 Fax 071-824 8865** is an elegant and professional antique dealer.

Como Lario

22 Holbein Place London SW1W 8NL Tel 071-730 2954

This is a completely unmodernized Italian restaurant, a London trattoria museum, immensely popular with locals who find comfort in its trenchant lack of affectation or charm. In complete contrast is **L'Incontro 87 Pimlico Road SW1W 8PH Tel 071-730 3663**, no more than 200 metres distant. This is the latest in a small succession of restaurants belonging to Gino Santini. Beginning humbly in Richmond, the Santini restaurants have evolved to define the upper limits of style, ambition and expense in Italian catering. The interior design by Peter Glyn-Smith is sharp, hard and knowing, grey and bright, giving a convincing impression of smartness and the suggestion – subsequently justified – that your wallet is going to be shredded. Food is vaguely Venetian, as is Santini. The wine list is maddeningly expensive and certainly not selected to be customer-friendly. A semi-good restaurant for a luxo-splurge dinner, but by no means the best Italian food in town.

La Poule au Pot

231 Ebury Street London SW1W 8UT Tel 071-730 7763

La Poule au Pot is a romantic restaurant, comfortable, dark and woody, with open fires in winter and lots of ooh-la-la *accueil* from the ethnic staff. It serves decent, old-fashioned bistro food.

Robert Day

89 Pimlico Road London SW1W 8PH
Tel 071-824 8655 Fax 071-730 7184
Sophisticated, intense flower arrangements and own-brand room sprays and fragrances, but you can also try the stand by Arne Jacobsen's Danish Embassy in Sloane Street, or the Toyota truck always parked in Belgrave Square.

Boucherie Lamartine

229 Ebury Street SW1W 8UT
Tel 071-730 3037
Boucherie Lamartine is the shop belonging to the Roux brothers, London's best-known French restaurateurs and the most encrusted with Michelin rosettes. Here you get chanterelles, *foie gras* and French cuts of meat (a *boucher* conceives and deconstructs a cow in an entirely different manner to a butcher), and all the fine produce you would expect at a first rate *traiteur*. Frighteningly expensive. Across the road, at 180 Ebury Street, Wolfgang Amadeus Mozart composed his first symphony.

As a pleasing counterpoint to the expensive, relaxed refinement of the antique village of Pimlico, **Peter's** taxi drivers' restaurant **59 Pimlico Road SW1W 8NE Tel 071-730 5991** has no equals. Huge, fat-rich English breakfasts served all day.

Chelsea Rare Books

313 King's Road London SW3 5EP
Tel 071-351 0950 Fax 071-351 2928
A relaxed, old-fashioned antiquarian bookseller with a small, but interesting stock that always changes. The proprietor, Leo Bernard, will negotiate.

Rococo

321 King's Road London SW3 5EP
Tel 071-352 5857 Fax 071-352 7360
A specialist shop selling imported Belgian and French chocolates (try Valrhona for a chocolate high), as well as locally hand-made varieties.

Gregor Schumi

317 King's Road London SW3 5EP
Tel 071-351 7537

Gregor Schumi is a fascinatingly lugubrious Austrian who briskly cuts anybody's (but especially starlets') hair with nothing but electric shears. No idle chit chat. Expensive.

La Tante Claire

68 Royal Hospital Road London SW3 4HP
Tel 071-352 6045 Fax 071-352 3257

The restaurant run by Pierre Koffmann, the author of *Memories of Gascony*, is one of London's most celebrated and in many ways the best, at least in the technical sense. Walk down Royal Hospital Road early enough in the morning and you will see refrigerated vans from Rungis and Boulogne delivering the best produce. Memories include not just goose fat and garlic, but dishes which combine robust flavours, sometimes juxtaposing fish and meat on the same plate. Restaurant is bright, modern and pastel-luxurious. Service is ultra-professional, but perhaps a little off-putting to the *ingénu*. Very stiff linen, good tableware. Lunch good value, especially on Wednesday, when the Physic Garden next door is open (see p.82).

Holmes Place Gym

188 Fulham Road London SW10 9PN
Tel 071-352 9452 Fax 071-376 3517

Completely straight, mixed gym, the best equipped in central London, with all the usual facilities, including a fine pool. The first stop for visiting Californian fanatics, Holmes Place is blessedly lacking locker-room jockstrap ambience. It is an expensive, smart, wholesome gym for people serious about keeping fit. Overseas visitors can negotiate short-term membership.

Chelsea Sports Centre

Chelsea Manor Street London SW3 5PL
Tel 071-352 6985

Provides similar facilities to Holmes Place, but with more local authority institutional ambience.

Pan Bookshop

158 Fulham Road London SW10 9PR
Tel 071-373 4997 Fax 071-370 0746

A medium-sized, eclectic – even anarchic – bookshop owned by the Macmillan Group and specializing in quality paperbacks. Unusually, it is staffed by knowledgeable and helpful assistants who understand books and reading habits. It is open until late and frequently does promotions and readings. An ideal place to spend half an hour before or after drinking beer in Finch's, or eating at Pizza Express, both of which are just across the road.

Lea & Sandeman

301 Fulham Road London SW10 9QH
Tel 071-376 4767 Fax 071-351 0275

Most London wine merchants are staffed by preening, condescending public schoolboys who regard customers as a health hazard. This is only a half-truth when applied to Lea & Sandeman, a start-up retail business with an astonishingly sophisticated and interesting range of wines, mostly from the Old World and full of curiosities and rarities. Opposite the Fulham Road Oddbins (a deservedly successful retail chain), Lea & Sandeman offers a step-ahead experience for the comfortably off wine-lover. Its list is the most fastidiously and intelligently presented in London; getting a copy is worth the journey itself. This is a better wine shop than you will find *anywhere* else in Europe.

Luigi's

349 Fulham Road London SW10 9TW
Tel 071-352 7739

Unusual for London in that it is open until 10.00 pm, Luigi's is the best Italian delicatessen in west London.

La Famiglia

7 Langton Street London SW10 0JL
Tel 071-351 0761 Fax 071-351 2409

Since 1964 La Famiglia has been a Chelsea landmark. Owner Alvaro Maccioni provided nightlife to a jaded 1950s' London, then returned to Tuscany to buy back land his family had lost, but grew restive in the country and came back to London. The unchanging menu and unchanging staff offer Tuscan specialities. Ask to taste the different bright green olive oils, and if you are hungry order *fantasia di pasta* or the *salsiccie* (sausages) which Alvaro makes from the wild boar he raises in Surrey. Otherwise, *panzanella* (bread soup) and *marietta di manzo* (barely warmed raw beef with garlic) are unique in London. Customers are smart Chelsea regulars; noisy indoors. Insist on a table in the garden in anything other than heavy rain. About £65 for two.

Blake's Hotel

33 Roland Gardens London SW7 3PF
Tel 071-370 6701 Fax 071-373 0442

Blake's is famous for a number of things. First, it is owned by the glamorous Sir Mark and Lady Weinberg (Anouska Hempel). Second, it is one of the only quality hotels outside the very centre of London. Third, it is very odd indeed. Blake's is the sort of hotel an exhausted Californian media lord would select as his first stop after Heathrow. It has an environment which positively purrs with the satisfaction of (new) wealth. Decor is hard to describe using conventional terms in architectural lexicology, but words such as rattan, lacquer and oriental come to mind. The food is equally schizoid, but excellent quality, although predictably expensive. The downstairs bar is a very good place for an elegant drink.

Pantalon Chameleon

Shop 3 Donovan Court Drayton Gardens London SW10 9QS Tel 071-835 1273 Fax 071-352 0340

Pantalon Chameleon is London's only business which declares itself to be a 'trouser specialist'.

Suzanne Ruggles

90 Fulham Road London SW3 6HR
Tel 071-584 3329 Fax 071-584 3329

Suzanne Ruggles is a designer of interesting, if sometimes overbearingly coy, wrought-iron furniture.

Conran Shop

Michelin House 81 Fulham Road London SW3 6RD Tel 071-589 7401 Fax 071-823 7015

Terence Conran did for British home furnishing what Mary Quant did for fashion and the Beatles for popular music: invigorated a lethargic local culture with a mixture of opportunism, eclecticism, inspired borrowing and a great deal of personal style. The Conran Shop is both the beginning and the end of the Conran retail story, which went from rags to riches to very great riches and back to riches again. With misguided megalomaniac expansion now behind it, the Conran Shop has resumed its role as a selling museum of contemporary style. There is simply nowhere better – anywhere in the world – to buy modern furniture, household and kitchen accessories. The place oozes optimism, conviction and relaxed stylishness. Saturday morning shopping there is like belonging to a vast cosmopolitan club dedicated to promenading; you see Loden coats and hear Italian spoken more often than you see tweed jackets or county drawls.

Bibendum

Michelin House 81 Fulham Road London SW3 6RD Tel 071-581 5817 Fax 071-823 7925

One of his partners once said of Terence Conran that he wants to give the world a better salad bowl. For twenty-five years he did more or less precisely that with his influential chain of Habitat shops (whose first store was just across the road in what is now Joseph), but since the late 1980s he has been concentrating on giving London better restaurants. Bibendum (from the motto 'Nunc est bibendum' – Now is the time to drink) is the showpiece of the Conran world. In a superbly airy and elegant arched space above the bustling, chic, cosmopolitan Conran Shop, the Bibendum interior was designed by Conran himself in the shell of the Michelin Tyre Company's old headquarters. It is generous and comfortable, understated but luxurious. Cooking projects Conran's own Anglo-French tastes, given a prodigious spin by the very talented and very committed chef/co-proprietor, Simon Hopkinson. Late in her life Elizabeth David was a regular customer, something which (quite correctly) Conran and Hopkinson regard as a great compliment. Bibendum is dedicated to David's adaptation of Escoffier's dictum, 'Faites simple!' For some, Hopkinson's cooking is too rich a simplicity: a vast sinew-free entrecôte might be served with marrow, *foie gras* and a dizzily intense reduction of wine sauce *and* horseradish made with cream, but for people who like eating very well in the company of the *beau monde* there is nowhere – anywhere – better. The wine list is breathtaking in every way, the whole experience very expensive, but very impressive. No compromise and not for the nervous.

Joseph

77 Fulham Road London SW3 3AH
Tel 071-823 9500 Fax 071-589 3571

Joseph Ettedgui is London's most brilliant fashion entrepreneur, and this is his best shop. A brilliant and constantly refreshed range of celebrity and own-name women's wear and men's wear (ground floor and basement repectively) is just the affordable side of expensive.

Joe's Café

126 Draycott Avenue London SW3 3AH
Tel 071-225 2217

Like the Joseph shop, designed by Anglo-Czech hardliner, Eva Jiricna, Joe's Café is somewhat like an art deco liner mated with the Pompidou Centre, a small masterpiece of 1980s' hard-edge interior design. It serves fashionable food with an emphasis on salads so that customers already weighted with shopping bags jammed with Moschino and Alaia need carry no unnecessary ballast. Best for coffee on Saturday mornings.

The Brasserie

272 Brompton Road London SW3 2AW
Tel 071-584 1668

The Brasserie is one of those restaurants which will probably last forever. Among the very first London restaurants to replicate the French formula for all-day dining and newspapers on sticks, fashions in food have long, long ago overtaken the Brasserie, although it is crowded from morning to night. Food is for retired taste buds, but the atmosphere is stimulating. The staff are implacable and never change.

Admiral Coddrington

17 Mossop Street London SW3 2LY
Tel 071-703 3273

A pub distinguished for nothing so much as being a favoured pick-up place for smart young Chelsea.

Moving down Fulham Road from Brompton Cross you pass **Elystan Street** on the left. This looks unprepossessing, but the bleak road that leads to Chelsea Green has some interesting shops which repay quiet attention.

Robert Stephenson

1 Elystan Street London SW3 3NT
Tel 071-225 2343

Stephenson is a discreet dealer in carpets and needlepoints.

WGT Burne

11 Elystan Street SW3 3NT
Tel 071-589 6074 Fax 081-944 1977

Burne is a specialist in antique English and Irish glass. There are no bargains, but the quality is consistent, expertise high and the prices accessible.

Lewis & Wayne

13-15 Elystan Street London SW3 3NT
Tel 071-589 5730

Lewis & Wayne is, by the common assent of all the very smart Chelsea ladies who take their dirty clothes there, London's very best dry cleaner. The firm's delivery vans, with the motto about cleaning to a standard, not a price, are familiar sights in SW's smart, tree-lined squares and avenues.

Sign of the Times

17 Elystan Street London SW3 3NT
Tel 071-589 4774

Those Chelsea ladies with wardrobes too tired for even Lewis & Wayne to revive take their Chanel, Armani, Rykiel, Sander, Gigli and Kenzo clothes to London's smartest second-hand clothes shop. Nothing in Chelsea is cheap, but if you arrive early there are sometimes astonishing discoveries.

Jane Asher Party Cakes

24 Cale Street London SW3 3QU
Tel 071-584 6177 Fax 071-584 6179

After a celebrity career in the 1960s, Jane Asher settled in Chelsea and wrote books about cakes. Her shop specializes in them, offering bravura essays in cake-mixture sculpture. Should you need a sponge in the form of a

Porsche 911 or a cellular telephone, or any other disguise, you will find it (or can have it made to order) here.

Manolo Blahnik

49 Old Church Street London SW3 5BS
Tel 071-352 3863 Fax 071-351 7314

Manolo Blahnik, half Czech, half Spanish, owns one of the most beautiful and strange shops in London, where he sells his strange and beautiful shoes.

The Front Page

35 Old Church Street London SW3 5BS
Tel 071-352 0648

One of the more salubrious and discreet Chelsea pubs.

Divertimenti

139-141 Fulham Road London SW3 6SD
Tel 071-581 8065 Fax 071-823 9429

A complete, professional, but rather joyless, kitchenware store.

Watch Gallery

129 Fulham Road London SW3 6RT
Tel 071-581 3239 Fax 071-584 6497

A specialist shop owned by Prince Ernst August of Hanover, a pretender to the English throne. Next door **Farah Lister 137 Fulham Road London SW3 6RT Tel 071-823 9878** sells inventive, sometimes contorted, jewellery.

Theo Fennell Ltd

175-177 Fulham Road London SW3 6JW
Tel 071-376 4855 Fax 071-376 4910

Theo Fennell is the jeweller favoured by the set that likes to have custom-made silver mascots of retrievers mounted on the bonnet of their Gloucestershire-registered, mud-stained BMWs. It is a very modern shop with a style of service and business attitude to match, selling defiantly unmodern jewellery. There is nowhere better to satisfy a hankering for diamond cluster, pearl-drop earrings. The neighbouring **Butler & Wilson 189 Fulham Road London SW3 6JN Tel 071-352 3045 Fax 071-376 5421** trades in a dramatically different style.

Papyrus

48 Fulham Road London SW3 6HH
Tel 071-584 8022 Fax 071-581 8908

Papyrus is a newcomer. London is surprisingly short of quality stationers.

Piero de Monzi

68-70 Fulham Road London SW3 6HH
Tel 071-581 4247

Piero de Monzi was selling fine Italian clothes in the dim ages before Armani. It is still a good place to buy elegantly conservative fashion for men and women.

Borgo San Frediano

62 Fulham Road London SW3 6HH
Tel 071-584 8375

After buying a cashmere cardigan or silk dress at Piero de Monzi, lunch at Borgo San Frediano is a pleasing period entertainment. The ambience is Chelsea in the 1960s, with rush chairs and red-painted tables. Noisy and reactionary, but smart in a subtle way.

Argenta

82 Fulham Road London SW3 6HR
Tel 071-584 1841 Fax 071-584 3119

Argenta has an intimidatingly drab street side, but carries an interesting range of modern jewellery. The staff are knowledgeable, helpful and resourceful; if they have not got what you want, they can make it.

American Classics

404 King's Road London SW10 OLJ
Tel 071-351 5229 Fax 071-376 7686

For those still keen to replicate the style of Eddie Cochran, this group of shops has an astonishing range of part-worn jeans, letter jackets and trucker's caps.

The pair of crescents known as **The Boltons** was built by George Godwin between 1850 and 1860; the church of St-Mary-the-Boltons sits in the space in between. At the time they were built, houses in The Boltons were among the most splendid in Britain, and they remain so today. The palatial scale, the urban conveniences and the rural feeling make this a uniquely British essay in town-planning. A blue plaque records that the painter Sir William Orpen lived at 8 South Bolton Gardens.

Le Suquet

104 Draycott Avenue London SW3 3AE
Tel 071-581 1785

A formula restaurant, but none the worse for that. A bit like a Marseilles theme park. Terrific range of interesting salads, but *plateau de fruit de mer* is the reason for a visit. Blustery, amiable French service.

Poissonnerie de l'Avenue

82 Sloane Avenue London SW3 3DZ
Tel 071-589 2457 Fax 071-581 3360

Very old-fashioned, which is to say pre-1980. Marine paintings, gueridons, chafing dishes and lots of cream. Old waiters, fresh fish. A feeling of inner calm, like being in the galley of a comfortable schooner long ago left adrift, but enjoyable. Not for the frivolous.

Chanterelle

119 Old Brompton Road London SW7 3RN
Tel 071-373 7390

Chanterelle is a museum piece. Originally owned by Baxter's the butchers, it was Terence Conran's first interior design commission and the source of the louvre in decoration. Now it is inhabited by comfortable Chelsea ladies. Very friendly prices, overwhelmingly homosexual staff, cosy, charming. In an attractive, low-built, red-brick building with stone dressing, very Brompton. Period bistro cooking; large portions for genteel clientele. Should last forever – looks as though it already has done.

Designer's Guild

271-277 King's Road London SW3 5UN
Tel 071-351 5775 Fax 071-376 4108

Tricia Guild's decorating shop is a window into a sharp, colourful, stylish soul. Designer's Guild has a fabulous range of furnishing fabrics, furniture and household accessories. It publishes a fine catalogue and provides consultancy services. Not for the ascetic or the minimalist, the style is indefinable polychrome, eclectic, Mediterranean, certainly it is *decorative*. For the comfort-loving, non-doctrinaire post-modernist with long pockets, the best decorating shop in London.

Osborne & Little

304 King's Road London SW3 5UH
Tel 071-352 1456 Fax 071-351 7813
Peter Osborne may be the first person ever to have been knighted for services to wallpaper. The King's Road shop has a range of fabrics and wallcoverings exerting a strong appeal to traditional taste. A short cab ride away **Ian Mankin 271 Wandsworth Bridge Road London SW6 2TX Tel 071-371 8825 Fax 071-722 2159** sells tougher, more restrained, more workmanlike tickings and other vernacular types.

Van Peterson

117A/9 Walton Street London SW3 2JD
Tel 071-589 2155 Fax 071-584 8165
Smart, modern jeweller.

San Martino

103 Walton Street SW3 2HP
Tel 071-589 3833 Fax 071-584 8418
A Walton Street classic, a robust 1960s' Italian (recently renovated and enlarged) in the middle of the swagged and draped desert of Chelsea-Knightsbridge decorators. Spaghetti in a bag is a dish the restaurant is proud of. Pushy service. Cool, tiled floors, but cramped and not very comfortable. Sometimes there is interesting game on the menu. Proprietor Costanzo Martinucci grows his own vegetables in a bizarre Tooting garden.

The Enterprise

35 Walton Street London SW3 2HU
Tel 071-584 3148 Fax 071-584 1060
A very comfortable and civilized converted pub offering a civilized menu to people wanting lunch at very un-pub prices. Food is well prepared but lies rather heavily on the stomach: it is possible, although certainly not desirable, to have *quesadillos* (cheese sandwiches) followed by salmon fishcakes and chips. Upper middle-class neighbours still treat the bar as their local.

Chelsea Physic Garden

Royal Hospital Road London SW3 4HS
Tel 071-352 5646

Open Wednesday and Sunday afternoons, April to October.
The garden was founded in 1673 by the Society of
Apothecaries of London from a gift by Sir Hans Sloane; it is
one of the oldest botanical research establishments, but
also one of great charm and beauty. Sloane's gift
depended on the condition that the apothecaries would
'keep it for the manifestation of the glory, power and
wisdom of God'. The US cotton industry began when seeds
were sent from Chelsea to America in 1732.

Royal Hospital

Royal Hospital Road London SW3 4SR
Tel 071-730 0161 Fax 071-823 6871

The hospital, built between 1660 and 1685, was founded by
Charles II when Nell Gwyn encouraged him to create a
retirement home for 400 veteran soldiers known as the
Chelsea Pensioners. Sir Christopher Wren was the
architect. The hospital graveyard, known as the Burial
Grounds, has been haunted since 1691. The grounds of the
Royal Hospital incorporate the old Ranelagh Gardens
pleasure grounds where milordi once paraded. On the other
side of Burton's Court, the private green space opposite the
Royal Hospital, is the house at 18 St Leonard's Terrace,
where Bram Stoker, author of *Dracula,* lived. Chelsea
Embankment, some 500 metres away, is the finest stretch
of Sir Joseph Bazelgette's monumental civil engineering
work on London's water systems, natural and man-made
(the capital's main sewers are below).

Carlyle's House

24 Cheyne Row London SW3
Tel 071-352 7087

The house is exactly as Thomas Carlyle, the austere
Scottish political economist, author of *The French
Revolution,* used it in later life, full of personal relics and
almost completely lacking in electricity. Here he entertained
leading High Victorian intellectuals, including Ruskin and
Dickens. Open Wednesday to Sunday from April to the end
of October.

Asparagus was first cultivated on the site of **Battersea Park**, laid out by Sir James Pennethorne with spoil from the creation of the Embankment. Once remote from the centre of London, Battersea Park was a favourite duelling spot; the Duke of Wellington and Lord Winchelsea were among the last to use it for this purpose. In 1985 missionaries from the Nipponzan Mohoyogi built a Buddhist temple of peace. The view from there to the opposite bank offers one of the finest vistas of urban residential development in the world - at least the equal of the over-rated and strident Manhattan skyline.

Battersea Power Station

Queenstown Road London SW8

Battersea Power Station is as well known as Battersea Dog's Home, but more elegiac and monumental. A superb design (1932–34) overseen by Sir Giles Gilbert Scott, who also designed the classic red phone box, it recalls a distant day when industry offered a prospect of excitement and romance. Long since disused, this vast building (sometimes said to be the biggest brick structure in the world) with its fluted chimneys treated as classical columns, was victim of ambitious, underfunded and shortlived development as showpiece of a theme park. It is now a crumbling ruin which no one can afford to deal with.

I Sardi

112 Cheyne Walk London SW10 ODJ
Tel 071-352 7534

A restaurant with a fabulous, intimate site on a picturesque street opposite the Thames *and* with a pleasing garden, although since parking is impossible, it has never achieved the popularity it deserves. I Sardi is a rare example of a Sardinian restaurant with an interesting range of specialities, some of which are convincingly authentic, although sometimes the preparation is a bit heavy-handed. It is always a treat to visit this restaurant, especially after a bracing walk along the Embankment.

I Sardi is just a short walk from 119 Cheyne Walk, where JMW Turner spent the end of his life as an eccentric, pseudonymous recluse called Mr Booth. This part of Chelsea is populated by literary and artistic ghosts. Cheyne Walk has had an extraordinary sample of famous residents:

George Eliot at 4; Dante Gabriel Rossetti at 16; Mrs Gaskell at 93; James Whistler at 96; Isambard Kingdom Brunel at 98; Hillaire Belloc and Walter Greaves at 104; Wilson Steer at 109; Sylvia Pankhurst at 120. A short distance away, 34 Tite Street was the home of Oscar O'Flahertie Wills Wilde until his arrest in 1895. It was decorated by EW Godwin, who also designed the Tower House at 44.

The Surprise

 6 Christchurch Terrace London SW3 4AJ Tel 071-352 4699

This is a picturesquely sited pub, and so is **The Phene Arms 9 Phene Street London SW3 5NY** **Tel 071-352 8391**. Nearby, 215 King's Road was the home of Thomas Arne who composed 'Rule Britannia'; 56 Old Church Street was the home of Scott of Antarctica. **The King's Head and Eight Bells 50 Cheyne Walk London SW3 5LR Tel 071-352 1820** is a riverside pub of better character than most.

Pizza Express

 45/56 Battersea Bridge Rd London SW11 3AG Tel 071-924 2774

This is one of the airier establishments in this impressive, budget-priced chain. A good place for lunch (and ask for the additional chilli oil) after walking in Battersea Park or before a visit to one of London's least known small pleasures, Battersea Old Church.

Battersea Old Church

 Battersea Church Road London SW11

A good, ordinary eighteenth-century brick church, somewhat in the Wren style, in a quiet riverside patch of South London affording the best view of the atrocious Chelsea Harbour development. In the west end is an oriel window with an armchair reputed to have belonged to JMW Turner. From this site Turner made many of his Thames sketches. The London house of the Forbes family, publishers of *Forbes Magazine* and owners of an aircraft called 'The Capitalist Tool', is nearby.

Harvey's

2 Bellevue Road London SW17 7EG
Tel 081-672 0114

Tempted sometimes to more involvement in the history of publicity than the history of cooking, Marco Pierre White, with his celebrity monographs and full-page ads endorsing Olympus cameras, is a daunting individual. Despite White's fearsome reputation for being a rude, argumentative, choleric, talented martinet, his restaurant and the food it serves are exquisite and surprising. The decor should be taken as a lofty joke; service is French and lubricated. Sited in a picturesque strip facing Wandsworth Common, Harvey's is way, way south of central London, but to many discriminating Londoners this is perhaps the best food in the entire city.

Bridgewater

739 Fulham Road London SW6 5UL
Tel 071-371 9033 Fax 071-384 2457

This is the retail outlet of the business run by the talented and whimsical couple Emma Bridgewater and Matthew Rice. Witty ceramics.

Kensington and Notting Hill

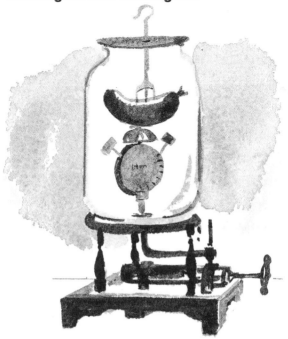

Notting Hill is the polite name for North Kensington. North and South Kensington are connected by Kensington Church Street, running down the west side of Kensington Gardens, past the Palace. Here are huge areas of stately terraces, with a royal character assumed by the High Victorian middle classes. The piety of Prince Albert and his legacy of museums and institutions affects the entire area with a feeling of institutionalised good will which evaporates the further north you travel through the borough towards the more 'colourful' Portobello Road. Architecturally, the style of the stucco houses was dramatically changed in the late nineteenth century when Richard Norman Shaw introduced his elegantly idiosyncratic buildings employing red bricks and stone dressings, influenced equally by the Dutch and by Queen Anne. Kensington provides the resources of the West End and Soho with the advantages of more breathing space and an unrivalled empire of museums.

Leighton House

12 Holland Park Road London W14 8LZ
Tel 071-602 3316 Fax 071-371 2467

Superb artist's house, designed for the painter Frederic Leighton in 1864–66 by his friend, the architect George Aitchison, in a remarkable high-rent artists' colony just off Kensington High Street; monumental Victorian redbrick egotistical swagger without, fabulously exotic Arabian pastiche within. You pass through a hall with dark blue tiles by William de Morgan into the Arab Hall, derived from a Moorish palace in Palermo. Blue and white tiles (mostly antiques collected by Leighton), tinkling fountains, major collection of Leighton's huge but vapid paintings, extravagant but pallid nudes, as well as works by Corot, Daubigny and English artist friends. Built as a home, a gallery and a studio (accurately preserved), Leighton House is a perfect introduction to the large-scale anomalies of late Victorian art and the perverse certainties of late Victorian taste. The quietness of the Leighton House garden is disturbed only by Leighton's own melodramatic sculpture of an *Athlete Struggling with a Python*. Nearby at 18 Melbury is the house the Pre-Raphaelite painter William Holman Hunt built for himself. Chaim Weizmann, one of the founders of modern Israel, lived around the corner at 67 Addison Road.

Linley Samborne House

18 Stafford Terrace London W4 1TT ·
Tel 081-994 1019/opening times from the
Victorian Society 081-995 4895

Linley Samborne (1844–1910) was one of the most prolific illustrators of the defunct magazine *Punch*. His house is preserved almost as he lived in it, not so much as a monument to his art (which neither required nor deserved such a grandiose gesture), but because it preserves the day-to-day living and working environment of a professional Victorian gentleman of artistic persuasion. In 1958 the influential Victorian Society was founded here by a group including Countess Rosse, Nikolaus Pevsner and John Betjeman.

L'Altro

210 Kensington Park Road London W11 1NR
Tel 071-792 1066

Kensington Park Road is a warm spot for restaurants.

L'Altro is the other half of Cibo, influential in its day. Interior design is absurd, with iconography as if an amateur dramatic society were putting on *Don Giovanni*. The effect is neither old nor new, and certainly not comfortable. L'Altro tends to concentrate on fish and insists on a Western-cosmopolitan reinterpretation of Italian peasant cooking completely unknown in Italy, but familiar to know-all food writers in New York and London. Lunch can be lonely; better for dinner if you have a sense of humour.

192

Kensington Park Road London W11 2ES
Tel 071-229 0482 Fax 071-727 7133

192 was one of London's first post-modern restaurants, which is to say that the interior design was confrontationally polychromatic and angular, denying customers the comfort of either modern beauty or old associations, but giving them a very clear view of architect Tchaik Chassay's aesthetic preoccupations. The kitchen was also post-modern, which in the gastronomic sense means it was not classical. The first cook here was the celebrated Alastair Little. His successors are perhaps not so fine or inventive, but adhere to his policy of eclecticism. This works only some of the time. Style, if that is not too dignified a word, tends to modern New York Cal-Ital. Service tends to be aggresso-sloppy. Not an absolute must, but better than most. Wine bar with food at street level; restaurant below stairs.

Kensington Place

201 Kensington Church Street London W8 7LX
Tel 071-727 3184 Fax 071-229 2025

Kensington Place is not perfect; it can be stiflingly noisy and the service is occasionally on the forgetful side of correct; the tables are close together, but at the same time the cavernous plan will deter agoraphobes. However, it is perhaps the very best restaurant in London – at once madly popular and full of the buzz of success, it is also relaxed and sophisticated with astonishingly non-aggressive prices. Julyan Wickham's adroit conversion of a mediocre 1960s' building at the Notting Hill end of Kensington Church Street provides the setting for a restaurant which can offer a light lunch taken on the breeze, or a more elaborate dinner. From the street the huge glazed façade offers a *tableau*

vivant of chattering, quaffing diners, rather like a human fish
tank. The chef, Rowley Leigh, is out of the School of Roux,
but his own style is much more modern. No nonsense
anywhere; free olives, good breads, good coffee. Menus
and wine list change frequently. Kensington Place is where
the up and coming and the down and going meet.

Clarke's

124 Kensington Church Street London W8 4BH
Tel 071-221 9225 Fax 071-229 4564

Clarke's is a celebrity restaurant in the good and the bad
senses. Its public is divided between those who are
slavishly adoring and those who think it over-rated.
Naturally, the truth lies somewhere between the two. The
menu is deliberately limited. This is more in the interests of
the proprietors than the customers since the motivation is to
cut down waste. Cooking is airy Californian, often char-
grilled, but sometimes pallid, although the materials are
always very fresh, a point of honour. Service can be
imprecise. The interior design perfectly complements the
cooking, being attractive, but not quite convincing: Clarke's
always has the feel of someone *pretending* to be running a
fine restaurant. Some will be irritated by the sanctimonious
atmosphere, others will find it exhilarating. The breads,
however, are superb and are available from the bakers and
deli next door, in some ways a better bet than the
restaurant, certainly at breakfast.

Victoria & Albert Museum

Cromwell Road London SW7 2RL
Tel 071-938 8500

The most magnificent museum of applied arts in the world,
a treasure house of such vast dimensions and wealth that
its occasionally careless keepers have no precise idea of
the range and depth of its collections – astonishingly, the
V&A has no catalogue. The vast Edwardian exterior by Sir
Aston Webb gives a misleadingly coherent look to an
institution whose plan has grown by accretion, accident and
mismanagement ever since the original South Kensington
Museum was founded to house the surplus from the Great
Exhibition of 1851. Recently brightened up from its
splendidly depressing gloom, the V&A is a cornucopia of art
and statistics; by some estimates there are fourteen miles
of exhibits. Certainly, it would take more than a lifetime to

become even flirtatiously acquainted with the collections. The most charming parts are perhaps the ones least influenced by the huge surge of modernization that took place in the 1980s. The medieval and early Renaissance exhibits are particularly wonderful, although the single most impressive room in the entire museum is perhaps the one intrinsically worth least: the cast courts, an astonishing testimony to High Victorian confidence, bluster and fakery. Go in there and sit with Browning or Tennyson for quarter of an hour and you can recapture the spirit of Victorian Britain in all its magisterial queasiness. An alternative focus would be the William Morris Room and the Poynter Room next door, the original restaurant. The present V&A restaurant is melancholy and should be avoided, no matter what state of desperation the visitor is in.

National Art Library

Victoria & Albert Museum Cromwell Road London SW7 2RL Tel 071-938 8315

The largest art library in Britain and one of the finest in the world, a magnificent memorial to Victorian confidence. Reader's tickets are required, but the library will issue them short term. A vast range of reference works are on open access, together with current periodicals, but the general stock is closed and requests have to be submitted on slips to the staff who are surly and discontented, but basically sound and efficient. The subject catalogue is a brilliant asset for anybody researching any area of the history of art. The library overlooks the museum's central garden; reading and writing there, in an atmosphere tangibly infused with the accumulated presence of great art, is one of life's keenest pleasures.

Brompton Oratory

Brompton Road London SW3 Tel 071-589 4811

It is astonishing to find a completely authentic Italian urban Baroque church in the centre of London – even the saints in the nave are from Siena. Designed by Herbert Gribble in 1878, the Oratory was the centrepiece of Cardinal Newman's oratory movement. It is now the centrepiece of Catholic society in Britain, *the* venue for fashionable weddings. Around the back there is a remarkable contrast with the stiff Anglican Gothic church of Holy Trinity and, beyond the pleasing gardens, a fine variety of characteristic London mews houses. Half an hour wandering this area can provide compelling examples of the variety and contrasts of British style and manners.

Natural History Museum

Cromwell Road London SW7
Tel 071-938 9123

The national collection of bones, fossils and stuffed animals housed in a gigantic municipal Gothic building by Alfred Waterhouse. Here is the scriptural home of palaeontology. The reason to go to the Natural History Museum, besides the experience itself – it is a museumpiece of a museum, the place where taxonomy was refined – is, above all, the dinosaurs. It was Richard Owen, first superintendent of the Natural History Museum, who was singly responsible. His article in *Journal of the British Association* in 1841 was where he coined the word 'dinosaur', a terrible lizard. The reconstitution by pioneer palaeontologists of old fossils and knuckle joints into creatures which haunt our imaginations is one of the great intellectual adventures of all time and it can be enjoyed best in the Natural History Museum. Atrocious restaurant.

Science Museum

Exhibition Road London SW7 2DD
Tel 071-938 8000

Built in 1913 to a design of Sir Richard Allison, during the marketing-driven explosion of low-voltage lights which constituted the museum 'revolution' of the 1980s, the enormous, sleepy Science Museum was first in the queue to get wired for pounds. The effect occasionally calls to mind a failed East European Disneyland. The range of exhibits is spellbinding, but generally unimaginatively and and unintelligently organized, most visitors' reactions being a mixture of bewilderment and profound fatigue. The aeronautical gallery is perhaps the best, although amateurs of eccentric museum labelling will find pleasure everywhere. Despite the gloss, the Science Museum is still a depressing place to visit, the air rank with the aroma of institutional lavatories.

Albert Memorial

Kensington Gardens London SW7

The Albert Memorial, right in front of the Albert Hall, is the greatest work of Victorian art, a monument to the unity of science and art which the Prince Consort made the subject of his short and busy life. Designed as a huge reliquary by Sir George Gilbert Scott after a competition which included proposals for an Albert Fountain (and a futile trawl of Europe's quarries to find a 500-foot monolith, the widowed Queen's first request), the memorial is a complex and ambitious allegory of the Victorian imperial vision of the past and the present. It is a hopelessly elegiac faux-masterpiece, a memorial to dated British values as much as to a dead German prince. Designed in about 1876 and completed twenty years later when it had to be protected by riot police, the antiquarian memorial is contemporary with the invention of the telephone, typewriter and automobile. It stands on the site of the original Crystal Palace.

Royal Geographical Society

1 Kensington Gore London SW7 2AT
Tel 071-589 5466

The society is in premises which began life as a private house designed by Norman Shaw in 1875. The Map Room is open on weekdays. Exhibits include Dr Livingstone's campaign chair and Scott of the Antarctic's snow glasses. **The Royal College of Organists**, just beside the Albert Hall, has a garish purple-blue sgraffitto façade.

Royal College of Music

Prince Consort Road London SW7 2BS
Tel 071-589 3643 Fax 071-589 7740

The college has two unique collections: one of instruments, which is open on Mondays and Wednesdays in term time, and another of portraits of musicians from all countries.

National Sound Archive

29 Exhibition Road London SW7 2AS
Tel 071-589 6603 Fax 071-823 8970

This is a museum of recorded sound.

Bistro 190

190 Queen's Gate London SW7 5EU

Tel 071-581 5666

Yet another formula restaurant by Anthony Worrall-
Thompson, a cook pleased to be photographed in leather
trousers. Mediterranean eclectic. There is an irritating policy
of no booking, unless a member of the 'club'. Bistro 190
can afford to show only mild enthusiasm for its customers
as it is in an area where decent food is hard to find.

Ognisko Polskie

55 Prince's Gate London SW7 2PG

Tel 071-589 4670 Fax 071-581 8416

The Polish Hearth Club is one of a handful of Polish
organizations in South Kensington. Lugubrious atmosphere,
but charmingly so. Another is the **Sikorski Museum 20
Prince's Gate London SW7 Tel 071-589 9249**, a
Polish military museum.

Daquise

20 Thurloe Street London SW7 2LT

Tel 071-584 4944

The reputation of Polish cooking in London rests, for good
or bad, with Daquise, close to South Kensington tube
station. Partly a café, with cakes served by truculent, but
apparently authentic, Slavic women, there is also a licensed
restaurant. There is good Polish and Czech beer, but
indifferent wine. The food is atrocious, but – one imagines –
authentic. On a rainy day Daquise has a magnificent
ambience – old Polish generals with sodden trenchcoats sit
and mope and steam. A must see, but best not to eat much.

Kensington Gardens

London W8

Apparently a western extension of Hyde Park, but in fact
much older, Kensington Gardens is one of the great open
spaces of London, encompassing palaces, formal gardens,
water features (including the famous Round Pond where
Percy Bysshe Shelley sailed toy boats made of banknotes)
and diversions for an eclectic range of visitors and residents
in 275 acres. The Broad Walk is famous. Kensington
Gardens, described by much-quoted but infrequently read
diarist John Evelyn as 'very delicious', has been open to the
public since the reign of James I; Samuel Pepys used to

dress up to walk here in the days when the English genuinely knew what a promenade meant. Kensington Palace, London home of the Princess of Wales, was designed by Sir Christopher Wren and Nicholas Hawksmoor in 1689 for William III and Mary II on the basis of an older building (Nottingham House) completed at the very beginning of the century: it defines the 'William and Mary' style. The State Apartments are open to the public, and the Court Dress Collection includes displays of the courtly dress ritual, as well as Lady Diana Spencer's wedding dress. In the grounds is The Orangery, a quintessential garden building where Queen Anne took tea, and which now serves excellent traditional tea and cakes. There are few better places to enjoy Earl Grey than in a sublimely proportioned pavilion perhaps by the maverick assistant to Wren, Nicholas Hawksmoor – a unique experience and one worth savouring, especially on a sharp, wintry day. Across the way in Hyde Park is one of London's more curious memorials. In 1880 the Duchess of Cambridge got permission to bury her dog at Victoria Gate; more than 800 pet owners followed her example.

Launceston Place

1A Launceston Place London W8 5RL
Tel 071-937 6912 Fax 071-938 2412

For the visiting amateur of social anthropology not privileged with an invitation to one of Kensington's finer private houses, a visit to Launceston Place provides an efficient substitute. The decor (in contrast to Kensington Place, which is under the same management) is superbly and convincingly domestic, the location is in one of London's more seemly village environments (Lord Snowdon's photographic studio is just around the corner). The atmosphere in Launceston Place changes subtly between lunch and dinner. At midday it tends to be full of smart Kensington business people and smart Kensington families; dinner is more intimate, even romantic. The food is very good, classic, only mildly adventurous. Launceston Place achieves a sense of easy excellence; one of London's very best restaurants and an essentially English one too.

Mon Petit Plaisir

33C Holland Street London W8 4LX

Tel 071-937 3224 Fax 071-738 7045

A recent spin-off from the old-established Mon Plaisir in Covent Garden, serving the sort of bistro food which disappeared in Paris long ago, but still haunts the gastro-imaginations of hungry Francophiles. Prettily sited in a quiet enclave off the miserable end of Kensington Church Street, Mon Petit Plaisir is staffed by real French people. The menu and wine list are very short, the interior uncomfortably cramped, but the food decent and reliable. Ambience can be a bit abrupt; not a restaurant for a great occasion, but always a small pleasure to visit.

Annie Russsell

1 Kensington Church Walk London W8 4NB

Tel 071-937 6403

This tiny establishment in a picturesque, traffic-free cut provides, in modest and personal surroundings, one of the best hairdressing services in London. Mostly for women, men are not excluded, but may feel uncomfortable.

Wodka

12 St Alban's Grove London W8 5PN

Tel 071-937 6513

It would be eccentric to come to London and seek out Polish cooking, but Wodka is a surprisingly good and interesting restaurant which, thankfully, is none too slavish in its ethno-orientation, although purists with a craving for shipyard *golonka* and bread made out of coal may be disappointed. In a very quiet backwater off busy and charmless Gloucester Road, Wodka has a well-illuminated, modern feel, although the interior design makes a few references to traditional Polish cafés such as once existed, one imagines, in Gdansk or Szczytno. A huge range of flavoured vodkas and interesting Polish beers is available. Food is well executed and on the safe side of robust. An amusing place for lunch on a wet day.

Scarsdale

Pembroke Square London W8

There is little to detain the fastidious or demanding along the expensive, crowded corridor of Kensington High Street, but at the opposite end to Church Street and near Leighton

House, hidden behind Edwardes Square, is one of London's best pubs. It is dark inside with roaring fires, unspoilt and unpretentious. Pleasant outside seating in appropriate weather.

Portobello Road

London W11

This is quintessential 'Notting Hill', the first and still the most cosmopolitan area of London, which gave its name to notorious 1950s' race riots, still continuing in slightly different forms. Portobello Road extends all the way from the badlands of North Kensington, now populated by Spanish and Portuguese immigrants (supported by some very authentic shops) to the smartnesses of Notting Hill Gate. Fridays and Saturdays Portobello Road hosts one of the world's largest flea markets and is best avoided; there is a general market daily, but antiques predominate on Saturday. More so than most markets, generations of gullible visitors have made it a very easy place to be had; only the very secure and very adroit should attempt purchases. Otherwise, for those with a taste for street life, Portobello Road provides a fantastic range of shops, bars, pubs and restaurants, and trembles between being a senseless-killing area and a gentrified locale of pseudo-realist shops. More refined antique shops are in nearby **Ledbury Road.**

First Floor

186 Portobello Road London W11 1LA
Tel 071-243 0072 Fax 071-221 8387

A restaurant above a pub, hopelessly crammed with bricolage, like an internalized model of the area itself. Similarly, the food is post-modern in its defiance of narrow regional styles. Better than you would imagine.

Galicia

323 Portobello Road London W10 5SY
Tel 081-969 3539

A wonderfully authentic Spanish restaurant, which is to say solemn and gloomy, but full of atmosphere. Lots of hard, dull lighting and dark wood, with real Spaniards mumbling and arguing around the tapas bar, Galicia is a delightful

amusement for a Sunday lunchtime, but the prudent will
have satisfied their basic hunger before arriving; the food is
not very good.

Brasserie du Marche aux Puces

349 Portobello Road London W10 5SA
Tel 081-968 5828

A dark establishment – a converted pub – at the rougher
north end of Portobello Road, offering modern eclectic
dishes which allow bizarre transnational menus, including
couscous and spotted dick, to be composed. Pleasantly
bohemian, with amiably gormless service.

Geale's

2 Farmer Street London W8 7SN
Tel 071-727 7528

An unpretentious fish and chip restaurant with a liquor
licence, popular with Kensington families gastro-slumming.

Costa's Grill

14 Hillgate Street London W8 7SR
Tel 071-229 3794

Costa's Grill would not photograph well. It has every
appearance of being a cheap and nasty café of the late
1950s, constructed out of materials once used to make
caravans and trailers, including the now rare wood-grain
laminate. It is in fact a splendid Greek restaurant, with a
quality of food a micron or two above the Hellenic norm.
Staff include the marvellously miserable father figure who
sits glumly by the cash register day in and day out. The
waiters are kind to children and have been there for years.
One of them is even called Praxiteles. Arrive early in
summer to get a table in the garden and eat and eat and
eat.

Coronet Cinema

103 Notting Hill Gate London W11 3LB
Tel 071 727 6705

Originally the Gaumont Theatre, the Coronet has a
marvellous Italian Renaissance-style façade and Louis
Seize-style interior; the neighbouring, but less opulent,
**Gate Cinema 87 Notting Hill Gate London W11
3JZ Tel 071-727 4043** runs art films in an appropriately
drab and depressing environment.

The **Ladbroke Estate** was planned as a mid-nineteenth century exercise in *rus in urbe* and a walk around Pembridge Square, Ladbroke Square or Chepstow Villas is an education in fine *haut-bourgeois* property development.

Some of the best Kensington antique shops include: **Haslam Whiteway Ltd 105 Kensington Church Street London W8 7LN Tel 071-229 1145** a Kensington dealer who specializes in late nineteenth-century and early twentieth-century classics of modern design from William Morris to Alvar Aalto; **John Jesse Ltd 160 Kensington Church Street London W8 4BN Tel 071-229 0312 Fax 071-229 4732** specializes in Art Nouveau and Art Deco. **Through the Looking Glass Ltd 137 Kensington Church Street London W8 7LP Tel 071-221 4026** specializes in elaborate gilt mirrors.

Christie's

85 Old Brompton Road London SW7 3LD Tel 071-581 7611 Fax 071-321 3321
The South Kensington branch of this major auction house is always busy churning over that unidentifiable brand of artefact located between cheap art and expensive junk.

Caffe Nero

66 Old Brompton Road London SW7 Tel 071-589 1760 Fax 071-581 1610
Stand-up, Milanese-style Italian café; continuous opera, unusually good coffee with *cantuccini* and *panini*.

Café Lazeez

93-95 Old Brompton Road London SW7 3LD Tel 071-581 9993
Interesting, incongruous, but rather good Modernist Indian restaurant. The menu breaks away from the clichés of Indian cooking with as much conviction as the interior design clings to the assumptions of 1980s' 'style'.

La Bouchée

56 Old Brompton Road London SW7 3DY Tel 071-589 1929
A feeding stop for the sullen or giggly French nymphette community which shops and grazes in the hinterland of the

Lycée Français, the French School in London.
Extraordinarily cheap.

Bute Street is architecturally undistinguished, but has an
attractive, villagey character and a handful of pleasing
shops.

Tridias

25 Bute Street London SW7 3EY
Tel 071-584 2330
A toy shop of quality and distinction.

Jeroboam's

24 Bute Street London SW7 3EX
Tel 071-225 2232
Jeroboam's has daily deliveries of French cheese from
Paris's Rungis market, but also sells a discriminating range
of French wines and quality English cheeses. Charming
service.

The French Bookshop

28 Bute Street London SW7 3EX
Tel 071-584 2840 Fax 071-823 9259
A modest specialist supplier to Lycée Français nymphettes
and satyrs, but a useful source for anyone hooked on naff
paperbacks.

Waterstone's

99-101 Old Brompton Road London SW7 3LE
Tel 071-581 8522
193-195 Kensington High Street London W8 6SH
Tel 071-937 8432 Fax 071-938 4970
Two Kensington branches of the excellent national chain
which pioneered the idea of bookselling and book buying
as civilized pleasures.

Coy's of Kensington

2A Queensgate Mews London SW7 5QJ
Tel 071-584 7444 Fax 071-584 2733
An intimidatingly superior garage, blue chip motor trade in a
smart mews, specializing in fine vintage cars. The sort of
place you will find a Hispano-Suiza or a James Young-
bodied Rolls-Royce Phantom II. Staff especially intimidating.

Bombay Brasserie

Courtfield Road London SW7 4QH
Tel 071-370 4040 Fax 071-385 1669

The Bombay Brasserie belongs to the Taj Group, one of India's most successful businesses, proprietors of Bombay's splendid Victorian Taj Hotel. For nearly ten years the Bombay Brasserie has been London's outstanding Indian retaurant, whose style and quality forced many reassessments of.'curry'. Built on an impressive scale (with a dramatic conservatory) in what was a rundown hotel, the Bombay Brasserie has a fixed-price buffet lunch; help yourself as many times as your system can sustain from steaming cauldrons of often unusual dishes. At night, which is best avoided, there is an absurd pianist and a shockingly expensive à la carte menu.

Trevor Blount

38 Harrington Road London SW7 3HL
Tel 071-584 0680

A small, personal gym specializing in the Pilates method, invented in the 1930s' by Joseph Pilates who fled to America when invited by Hitler to train the German army.

Lidgate

110 Holland Park Avenue London W11 4UA
Tel 071-727 8243 Fax 071-229 7160

London's best butcher and game dealer with organic or grass-fed beef, real sausages, and terrines made with as few E-numbers as possible.

Bernard J. Shapero

80 Holland Park Avenue London W11 3RE
Tel 071-493 0876 Fax 071-229 7860

A good all-round antiquarian bookshop, tending to be expensive.

Books for Cooks

4 Blenheim Crescent London W11 8DY
Tel 071-221 1992 Fax 081-586 3886

A fabulous shop of old and new cookbooks with exemplary staff. A battered sofa does nothing to discourage browsing, and at the back of the store there is a small kitchen serving good coffee and cakes or light lunches. For anybody interested in food, Books for Cooks is a superb, civilized haven in a tiring area.

Travel Bookshop

13 Blenheim Crescent London W11 2EE

Tel 071-229 5260 Fax 071-243 1552

An excellent selection of old and new travel books.

Minus Zero Records

2 Blenheim Crescent London W11 1NN

Tel 071-229 5424

Specialist supplier for the too-old-to-rock too-young-to-die generation.

Khan's

13-15 Westbourne Grove London W2 4UA

Tel 071-727 5420

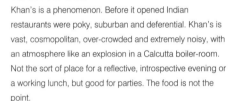

Khan's is a phenomenon. Before it opened Indian restaurants were poky, suburban and deferential. Khan's is vast, cosmopolitan, over-crowded and extremely noisy, with an atmosphere like an explosion in a Calcutta boiler-room. Not the sort of place for a reflective, introspective evening or a working lunch, but good for parties. The food is not the point.

L'Accento Italiano

16 Garway Road London W2 4NH

Tel 071-243 2201

L'Accento is the paradigm of new-wave Italian restaurants. *Pane integrale* and bright green oil instead of *grissini* or the sort of powder-dry *panini* which explode in a cloud of dust and fragments. Amiable service from well-dressed and well-meaning staff; a sort of gutsy Tuscan simplicity to the decor. Coarse, but pleasing, cooking. Inexpensive and deservedly very busy.

Bernadout & Bernadout

7 Thurloe Place London SW7 2RX

Tel 071-584 7658

Oriental rugs.

Hyper-Hyper

26-40 Kensington High Street London W8 4PF

Tel 071-938 4343

A covered new-clothes market, which includes Flying Down To Rio and Thunderpussy for the immature and those who couldn't care less.

Kensal Green Cemetery

Harrow Road London W10
Tel 081-969 0152

This is in a grim area along the depressing Harrow Road, some way out of visitors' London, but for the amateur of the macabre or the scholar of Victorian death ritual, it is a unique fantasy world. Opened in 1833, at the very beginning of the Victorian era, by the General Cemetery Company, there is, among the intensely picturesque and melancholy overgrown tombs, a Greek Revival chapel designed by Sir JD Paul, chairman of the board.

Lou Pescadou

241 Old Brompton Road London SW5 9HP
Tel 071-370 1057

One of the chain of Frenchified fish restaurants, mostly rather pleasing, owned by entrepreneurial Pierre Martin. This Earl's Court expression of the theme is expressly Provençal, although dingily so. There are real French waiters and an oddly depressing shelf of liqueurs, including neglected period pieces such as Drambuie. Still, with its woven plastic rush chairs there is a fragile sense of being in a *real* French café (with fisherman's balls and lacquered lobster shells).

The City, Docklands and the Southeast

The City of London, financial centre of the world, is a distinct
square mile that keeps office hours. Evenings and weekends it
is deserted and ideal for romantic walks past the idiosyncratic
architecture of Wren, Hawksmoor and Rogers. The City begins
at Aldwych, west end of Dr Johnson's "Grub Street". At Holborn
Bars is London's sole remaining medieval shop front. Johnson
lived here 1759-1760 and wrote his exotic satire *Rasselas* to
meet the costs of his mother's funeral. A network of alleys and
courts between Cornhill and Lombard Street are a reminder of
the old City which ends at Whitechapel where East London
begins. George Gissing described working-class London as a
"city of the damned". Now it is a city of the redundant. Once a
working river, the docks had closed by the seventies. Revived
with messianic enthusiasm (and a measure of short sight) in
the eighties, the London Docklands Development Corporation's
phantasmagoric renewal programme has been only partially
realised, giving London the planet's newest deserted city.
Canary Wharf destroyed the old Chinatown, but the terrifying
St. Anne's, Limehouse, inspiration of Peter Ackroyd's spooky
novel, *Hawksmoor* (1985) remains aloof from recent changes.

George and Vulture

3 Castle Street London EC3V 9DL
Tel 071-626 9710

This pub offers weekday lunch in extremely, some would say overbearingly, atmospheric surroundings, as does **Simpsons of Cornhill 38 1/2 Cornhill London EC3V 9DR Tel 071-626 9985**

Le Poulbot

45 Cheapside London EC2Y 6AR
Tel 071-236 4379

Long one of the City's only decent restaurants, Le Poulbot is best for breakfast. Excellent coffee and croissants.

Public Record Office

Chancery Lane London WC2
Tel 081-876 3444 Fax 081-878 7231

Has documents illustrative of Britain's decline from the magisterial Domesday Book to the shit-kicking minutiae of modern Cabinet papers. Just off Chancery Lane is **Carey Street**, notorious as the final destination of bankrupts.

Dr Johnson's House

17 Gough Square London EC4A 3DE
Tel 071-353 3745

This foursquare Georgian house was the home of the great lexicographer. It is close to **The Cheshire Cheese 48 Crutched Friars London EC3N 2AP Tel 071-488 1164**, one of Johnson's favoured inns.

Hatton Garden

London EC1

The area is famous as the diamond merchant and jewellery centre of London.

Leather Lane Market

London EC1

Lunchtime market close to Hatton Garden.

Quality Chop House

94 Farringdon Road London EC1R 3EA
Tel 071-837 5093

An extremely uncomfortable new restaurant enjoying something of a cult. Kitsch in its sly knowingness, this workman's caff has now been translated into a lunch-time yuppie haunt. It serves modishly proletarian food.

The Eagle

159 Farringdon Road London EC1
Tel 071-837 1353

One of a new breed of pub converted from smoky nastiness to meet the expectations of a younger clientele with horizons set more distantly than the bottom of the glass. Upstairs is a gallery. On the catering (ground) floor the seediness of a City pub has been almost completely replaced by something brighter, more wholesome and optimistic (although many attractive architectural features remain). The place is noisy from *Guardian* newspaper regulars. Food is modern Italianate.

HMS Belfast

Morgan's Lane Tooley Street London SE1 2JH
Tel 071-407 6434

A floating exhibit of the Imperial War Museum, HMS *Belfast*, a participant in the Battle of the River Plate, is a rare example of a surviving battleship. Its cramped, austere, frightening interior makes an astonishing contrast with the airy spaces of Hay's Galleria opposite. It is available for macabre private parties.

Museum of Garden History

St Mary-at-Lambeth Lambeth Palace Road
London SE1 7JU
Tel 071-261 1891 Fax 071-401 8869

A charmingly amateurish museum, laid out by what might be the Townswomen's Guild, but the larger meanings are impressive – a memorial to the magnificent Tradescants, gardeners to Charles I and Henrietta Maria. There is a replica seventeenth-century garden. The tomb of William Bligh, famous from his role in the mutiny on the *Bounty*, is in the graveyard.

Imperial War Museum

Lambeth Road London SE1 6HZ
Tel 071-416 5000 Fax 071-416 5374

The late Georgian building (with a dome added by Sir Sydney Smirke in 1844) was the second home of the notorious Bethlehem Hospital, which gave its name to the institution and condition of 'Bedlam', the subject of the last scene in Hogarth's pictorial morality tale, *The Rake's Progress*. Inside there is not only a fine collection of aircraft and weapons, together with some rather dubious sensoramas of First World War trenches and the Second World War blitz, but rather more importantly a superb collection of paintings and sculptures, including works by Nash, Severini and Epstein. The bulk of this is in reserve, but available for viewing by appointment.

 Westminster Bridge offers exceptionally fine views of London, the ones that inspired Wordsworth to write 'Earth has not anything to show more fair/Dull would he be of soul who should pass by/A sight so touching in its majesty', but in fact nowadays the view east from Waterloo Bridge is the more breathtaking. The stretch of the Albert Embankment running on the south side of the river between Westminster and Lambeth Bridges gives a very fine view of the Houses of Parliament and offers the opportunity for a very pleasant short stroll.

Hayward Gallery

 **South Bank Centre Belvedere Road
London SE1 8XZ
Tel 071-928 3144 Fax 071-928 0063**

If Britain had commissars of culture, they would preside here in this unloved, grimy concrete megastructure. The Hayward Gallery, chief feature of what is now known as the South Bank Centre, is devoted to temporary exhibitions of (mostly modern) fine art. A classical brutalist structure, it has more enemies than friends, especially because the exhibition programme is continuously suggestive of a hectoring, official, late mixed-economy version of what's good for you in contemporary culture. No one could find the buildings beautiful, but seen in the best possible light, which, given Thames-side conditions, happens only very rarely, they are bracingly urban and unashamedly 1960s'. In the same complex you will find the **National Film Theatre**, the **Queen Elizabeth Hall** and the **Purcell Room**.

National Theatre

Upper Ground London SE1 9PX
Tel 071-928 2252

Sir Denys Lasdun's National Theatre is trenchantly modernist and not much admired from outside, but within it is a masterfully organized labyrinth of satisfyingly complicated spaces. Three auditoria are united by interesting devices. Despite the brutal concrete and the complete want of concession to frivolity, the National Theatre interiors are warm, humane and attractive, good places to be... irrespective of whether you are going to see a play.

Royal Festival Hall

Belvedere Road London SE1 8XX
Tel 071-928 8800

In strong contrast to the National Theatre, Sir Leslie Martin's RFH is a masterpiece of 1950s' architecture, a built expression of the sensibilities of the Britain-Can-Make-It to You've-Never-Had-It-So-Good era. Classical and elegant, it has marvellous internal spaces.

Operating Theatre Museum and Herb Garrett

9A St Thomas Street London SE1 9RY
Tel 071-955 4791

This fragment of the old St Thomas's Hospital is a refreshingly gruesome reminder of the pleasures of progress.

Temple of Mithras

Queen Victoria Street London EC4

Visible from the street, this is a reconstruction of fragments found near this site. Mithras was the Roman equivalent of the Persian sun god, Zoroaster. A locale of melancholy charm.

Telecom Technology Showcase

135 Queen Victoria Street London EC4V 4AT
Tel 071-248 7444/071-236 5464

The video of the 1930s' film *The Fairy of the Phone* has great period charm.

The Blackfriar

174 Queen Victoria Street London EC4V 4DB
Tel 071-236 5650

An Arts and Crafts pub (1897) by H Fuller-Clark, an
overblown parody of all the tacky, unhealthy medievalism of
William Morris and his followers. A cocktail of marble,
bronze, mosaic and stained glass, The Blackfriar is not a
work of architectural genius – the design is far too self-
conscious and archly historicist – but a unique Victorian
theme pub.

St Bride Printing Library

Bride Lane London EC4Y 8EE
Tel 071-353 4660 Fax 071-583 7073

A run-down establishment with all the depressing hallmarks
of administrative neglect, but a superb archive and library of
typography, print and related trades.

Bracken House

near St Paul's Cathedral Cannon Street
London EC4

The old headquarters of the *Financial Times* in the days when
it was feasible and desirable to have editorial and print in
one building. Designed as late as 1956 by the redoubtable
Sir Albert Richardson, author of *Monumental Classical
Architecture in Britain and Ireland*, it was the first post-war
building to be listed. Sold to Japanese developer Ohbayashi
in 1986, the building has recently been eviscerated with
great taste by humane modernist Michael Hopkins.

Museum of the Order of St John

St John's Gate London EC1M 4DA
Tel 071-253 6644

This is a gloriously eccentric corner of Clerkenwell, a City
area with strong Italian and Mediterranean associations.
Housed in St John's Gate, once the entrance to the Priory of
Clerkenwell, it was built in 1504 and restored, although
some would say over-restored, in 1846. This is the sciptural
home of the Most Venerable Order of St John, a twelfth-
century religious order which cared for the sick. The modern
St John Ambulance Brigade spun off from this medieval
starting point, and there is a separate museum devoted
to the Brigade's activities. A late fifteenth-century
Netherlandish triptych showing *St John the Baptist*,

The Presentation of Christ in the Temple, *The Holy Trinity* and *The Presentation of the Virgin*, once the property of John Weston, who was Prior of the order from 1476 to 1489, is the outstanding single work of art. A collector's piece among small museums.

National Postal Museum

King Edward Street London EC1A 1LP
Tel 071-239 5420 Fax 071-600 3021

There is something powerfully elegiac about seeing some of the *very first* ever stamps and stamped letters. The National Postal Museum includes them among one of the world's outstanding philatelic collections. The most interesting way to approach the museum is through the odd and moving **Postman's Park**, just off St Martin's-le-Grand. This curious small park has a wall of plaques dedicated to heroic Londoners who met untimely ends in acts of spontaneous bravery. Office workers now incuriously eat sandwiches there at lunchtime.

Sweetings

39 Queen Victoria Street London EC4N 4SA
Tel 071-248 3062

This quaint City eating house makes boys familiar with brutal public schools feel at home. A noisy, antique fish restaurant with more character than charm, Sweetings is a treat for masochists and voyeurs. There is no booking, and to have even a slight chance of sitting down and eating you have to arrive before twelve. It can be hard on the nerves, but the quality of fish is good and the white wines served startlingly cold by brusque waiters.

Spanish and Portuguese Synagogue

Bevis Marks 2 Heneage Lane London EC3
Tel 071-626 1274

This is one of the oldest synagogues in London. The architect-builder was Mr Avis, a Quaker, who handed back his professional fee as a gesture of goodwill.

St Giles Cripplegate

87 Worship Street London EC2A 2BE

This is the burial place of John Milton, poet of *Paradise Lost*.

Broadgate

London EC2

Broadgate is the largest property development in Britain, a monument to 1980s' optimism and to the fast-track methods of construction developed by large American architectural practices. Broadgate is distinguished because it is a rare example of contemporary architecture to have won approval from the Prince of Wales, perhaps because the developers made certain concessions to the public, including the provision of bars, shops and works of art (including a monumental piece by minimalist sculptor Richard Serra).

Stephen Bull's Wine Bar and Bistro

71 St John Street London EC1M 4AN
Tel 071-490 1750

Harsh, modern decor. State-of-the-art modern restaurant cooking, mixing audaciously accurate technique with peasant recipes and fine-quality materials. Reasonable prices, not particularly relaxing.

John Wesley's House and the Museum of Methodism

49 City Road London EC1Y 1AU
Tel 071-253 2262

The founder of Methodism lived in this austerely elegant Georgian house just off the noisy, scruffy City Road (above the astonishing Finsbury Square, the only part of London that looks like the Mid-West), from 1779 to his death in 1791. Its architecture and fastidious state of preservation are symbols of the regular and respectful habits cultivated by Methodists. Wesley might have desribed it as 'neat but not fine'. The house is full of touching and quaint Wesleyana, including his hat and his library. There is something appealingly humane about these personal effects, especially when seen in the context of the Prayer Room where Wesley began each day at four 'far from the busy ways of man'. His tomb is in the small graveyard behind the chapel.

Lloyds

Lime Street London EC3M 7HA
Tel 071-623 7100 Fax 071-626 2389

Sir Richard Rogers' magnificent temple of lucre, a sophisticated casino designed on a system of hi-tech modules. Huge atrium; the effect can be unsettling since it is both delicate and heavy-handed, exhilarating, but overpowering. Users hate it, but it is one of the world's most remarkable modern buildings. It is said that the michievous Rogers got the plan approved by presenting a model in *wood* to the competition committee. Within Lloyds there is the Nelson Collection, a small museum of artefacts belonging to Admiral Horatio Nelson, and memorials to Lloyds' marine associations. The building itself has a public viewing gallery.

Leadenhall Market

London EC3 Tel 071-260 1530

Just around the corner from Lloyds is Leadenhall Market, designed and built in 1881 by Horace Jones, architect of Tower Bridge. A cruciform stone and glass Victorian interpretation of the European *galleria*, with game dealers, fishmongers and wine merchants, Leadenhall Market has a distinctive artistic exuberance and commercial vitality, very different from the sobriety of other Victorian City institutions.

St Stephen's Walbrook

Walbrook London EC4

Here is a chance to savour other contrasts and conflicts between old and new architecture. The church is one of Sir Christopher Wren's very greatest designs, an interior of fine complexity and subtlety combining all the elements of classical architecture into one building, which the great architectural historian, Nikolaus Pevsner, described as polyphonic. The church has, however, been criticized by other architectural historians for lacking a culminating feature. This was remedied when, in the course of restoration which he sponsored, Lord Palumbo of Walbrook installed a monumental Henry Moore altarpiece, likened by hostile commentators to an unripe Camembert cheese. The dome of St Stephen's is a prototype for St Paul's.

Mappin & Webb

2 Queen Victoria Street London EC4N 4TL
Tel 071-248 6661 Fax 071-248 3839

Opposite St Stephen's Walbrook, is a memorial to a failed ambition and the most vexatious site in modern London, with a famously rejected design by Mies van der Rohe and a more recent design by Sir James Stirling, which is also in dispute. Sir Edwin Lutyens' **Midland Bank 89 Queen Victoria Street London EC4V 4AQ Tel 071-236 5691 Fax 071-248 3649** in Poultry was, until Sir Richard Rogers' Lloyds Building, the most significant twentieth-century building in the City.

City Club

 Old Broad Street London EC2

This is a classic of 1830s' Roman palazzo style by Philip Hardwick, architect of the famously demolished Euston Arch.

St Mary Woolnoth

 Lombard Street London EC3V 9AN Tel 071-626 9701

This is one of the most brilliantly original designs by Nicholas Hawksmoor, Wren's chief assistant, whose reputation for perverse and dramatic genius made him the subject of Peter Ackroyd's bravura novel *Hawksmoor*. It is a masterpiece of the English Baroque, intellectual and restrained and intensely personal when compared to the continental.

Clockmaker's Company Collection

 The Clock Room Guildhall Library Aldermansbury London EC2P 2EJ Tel 071-6060 3030 ext1865

One of London's quaintest museums, ideal for introspection on the nature of flying time after a bibulous City lunch. Contains a collection of timepieces made by members of the company since 1631.

Bank of England Museum

 Threadneedle Street London EC2R 8AH Tel 071-601 4387 Fax 071-601 5460

The Bank – the Old Lady of Threadneedle Street – was one of the first of its kind in the world and has been on this site since 1694. It achieved its most magnificent architectural state during the rebuilding by Sir John Soane which turned it into a magnificently austere Romantic-Classical monument. The building has since been considerably mutilated, especially by Sir Herbert Baker during the thirties, but you can visit a reconstruction of Soane's original banking hall. At the same time, the changing fortunes of sterling have altered the status of the old lady, now more pompous than magnificent. There is a small museum of artefacts and documents on the history of the Bank.

HM Customs and Excise Museum

Custom House Lower Thames Street
London EC3R 6EE
Tel 071-283 5353

By appointment only, but worth it for the vicarious, masochistic experience of smuggling and excise.

The Monument

Monument Street London EC3 8AH
Tel 071-626 2717

A Doric column as *the* Monument to the Great Fire of 1666, designed by Sir Christopher Wren and built 1671–77. Its height of 202 feet is the distance from the column to the supposed source of the fire in Pudding Lane. There is an allegorical bas relief by Caius Gabriel 'Colly' Cibber. Climb the 311 stairs *before* a City lunch in **Bill Bentley's 1 St George's Lane off St Botolph's Lane London EC3 8DR Tel 071-929 2244** – there is no resting place on the ascent.

All Hallows-by-the-Tower

Byward Street London EC3R 5BJ
Tel 071-481 2928 Fax 071-488 3333

Historical records in this church (whose site has been in continuous use for 1300 years) include the baptism of William Penn and the marriage certificate of John Quincy Adams, sixth president of the United States.

Design Museum

Butler's Wharf 28 Shad Thames
London SE1 2YD
Tel 071-403 6933 Fax 071-378 6540

The Design Museum was opened in 1989 by Margaret Thatcher, the first prime minister to express an interest, perhaps misunderstood, in industrial design. Funded by the Conran Foundation, the Design Museum is one of the only museums in the world to be single-mindedly devoted to mass-produced consumer design. It has a permanent collection of noteworthy design, as well as temporary exhibition spaces and a reference library.

The dramatic, white building was fashioned from an undistinguished 1950s' warehouse. Within the museum is the **Blueprint Café Tel 071-378 7031** with a terrace and spectacular views of the river and City. It is an exciting, but not particularly comfortable, place to be. Cooking is Cal-Ital.

Le Pont de la Tour

Butler's Wharf London SE1 2YE
Tel 071-403 8403 Fax 071-403 0267

Some nights the (rather archly named) Pont de la Tour looks like *the* destination restaurant for Essex limo folk in costume jewellery on wobbly heels who don't make it as far as the West End. Alternatively, well-heeled tourists are on display. It is a huge and beautiful space (divided into a formal restaurant and a more relaxed bar and grill), with heartstopping views of Tower Bridge, day or night. The cooking is Frenchified and not as reliably impressive as the interior design – a dish of *tete de veau* was once recognisable, but the atmosphere is very buzzy, more New York than London. It is a glamorous place at night, more sober and businesslike at lunch time when City functionaries cross the bridge to the only decent restaurant in the area. As in all Terence Conran's restaurants, there is masses of comfortable style and interesting detail and a theoretical commitment to good wine and excellent cooking of quality ingredients which is sometimes breached in practice. Pont de la Tour is a bright and giddy success. It's just a pity that the food isn't always brilliant.

Cantina del Ponte

36C Shad Thames London SE1
Tel 071-403 5403

This restaurant is next door to the Pont de la Tour, among a cluster of small Thames-side institutions (including a wine merchant and a fishmonger) dedicated by Terence Conran to the goddess Cibo. The Cantina is Mediterranean generic, with a simple interior of hard furniture (tables by Conran himself) and an ambitious mural. It is the sort of place you find char-grilled calamaris salad or chick peas blended with porcini. The service is amiably relaxed, not to say undisciplined, and there is very good wine by the glass. Moderate prices and good fun.

Bloom's

90 Whitechapel High St London E1 7RA
Tel 071-247 6001

Bloom's is London's best-known kosher restaurant, in Jack-the-Ripper territory on the fringes of the City. The belligerent and surly staff is Cypriot, and through the custom of having to *buy* the dishes from the kitchen and sell them on to the customers, has acquired a richly deserved reputation for hustling. Ambience is like a Rumanian penal institution, as different from a decent New York Jewish deli as you could imagine, but Bloom's is perfectly sited to satisfy a rich craving for chopped liver, gefilte fish and poor Israeli wine after a visit to the spare Whitechapel Art Gallery.

Whitechapel Art Gallery

80 Whitechapel High Street London E1 7QX
Tel 071-377 0107

Landmark Art Nouveau design by C. Harrison Townsend, recently refurbished with great taste by Colquhoun and Miller. The gallery used to have a reputation for brave shows about difficult modern artists, but the wave of popularly-driven revisionism in art criticism and appreciation has recently combined with lacklustre direction to make the gallery a stranded anomaly. Still, it is worth going to see whatever is on to enjoy the building.

Dennis Severs' House

18 Folgate Street London E1 6BX
Tel 071-247 4013

Spitalfields, home to a succession of immigrants, including Huguenots, Ashkenazim Jews, Bengalis and more recently architectural enthusiasts in rotting tweeds, has some houses of quality which provide the clearest idea of what pre-industrial London looked like. A walk along Brick Lane, with its sari shops and grim Indian cafés, gives a similar vision of post-industrial London. Dennis Severs has made his own house into a high camp tableau-vivant of the fictional Jarvis family. An amusing distraction for credulous voyeurs.

Geffrye Museum

Kingsland Road London E2 8EA
Tel 071-739 9893 Fax 071-729 5647

Way, way off the usual museum drag, the Geffrye Museum offers a splendid experience of high-brow voyeurism to the intrepid traveller or curious amateur. It dates from 1914, when a 1715 almshouse was converted into a museum of the furniture trade. It contains the diarist John Evelyn's Cabinet of Curiosities, a bizarre, instructive collection of shells, stuffed animals and odds and ends. Since 1939 the museum has concentrated on building scholarly, authentic (but also moving and fascinating) sets illustrative of the history of that terrible institution – the British front room. A superb and witty museum of middle-class taste.

Billingsgate

Lower Thames Street London EC3

The old fish market, source of many Cockney myths and fishy tales. According to Henry Mayhew in his classic *London Labour and the London Poor* (1861), it was a perfect Babel of competition. Its present circumstances eloquently project the changing fortunes of the City. Its riverbank site used to provide a real mercantile counterpoint to the more abstruse and abstract financial dealings of the City, a contrast which used to give London such character. Now the market has been abandoned (the fishmongers left for the Isle of Dogs in 1982) and Lower Thames Street is now a thundering four-lane traffic jam. The old building, with its elaborate exterior and dignified interior spaces, has been converted to modern commercial use by Sir Richard Rogers, architect of the Lloyds Building. The best view is from the South Bank.

One Canada Square

London E14

Cesar Pelli's monumental high-rise at Canary Wharf is one of the most complete and affecting memorials of the 1980s. The ruin of its Canadian developers, Olympia & York, Canary Wharf is full of the melancholy of all abandoned ideal cities; here on the Isle of Dogs thoughts of Angkor Wat and Arc-et-Senans come to mind.

Three classic riverside pubs are: **Prospect of Whitby 57 Wapping Wall London E1 9SP Tel 071-481 1095 Fax 071-481 9537**, where JMW Turner drank, and there is an upstairs restaurant; **The Angel 101 Bermondsey Wall East London SE16 4NB Tel 071-237 3608** also has an upstairs restaurant, and a balcony jettied out over the river; **The Grapes 76**

Narrow Street London E14 8BP Tel 071-987 4396 is the pub that Dickens used as the model for the inn in *Our Mutual Friend*.

Fan Museum

6 Turnpin Lane London SE10 9JA
Tel 081-305 1441 Fax 081-293 1889

A major collection of fans from the seventeenth century.

Shakespeare Globe Museum

Bear Gardens Bankside Liberty of the Clink London SE1 9EB
Tel 071-928 6342 Fax 071-928 7968

The most famous museum that has never been built. Nearby is Giles Gilbert Scott's magnificent **Bankside Power Station**, like its sibling at Battersea now off the national grid, but in better condition. Right next door is the house where Sir Christopher Wren lived while building St Paul's – one of the best sited in London.

St George-in-the-East

The Highway London E1
Tel 071-481 1345

A fine, dramatic English Baroque church by Thomas Archer.

Queen's House

Park Row London SE10 9NF
Tel 081-858 4422 Fax 081-312 6632

In all of Wren's magnificence, the earlier exquisite Queen's House stands out. To some, Inigo Jones designed the most beautiful house in Britain, certainly one of the most elegiac. Built in 1616 and now a part of the National Maritime Museum.

Old Royal Observatory

Blackheath Avenue London SE10
Tel 081-858 1167 Fax 081-312 6632

The Observatory is housed in Sir Christopher Wren's Flamsteed House of 1675, which provides one of the best views of Greenwich's Royal Naval College. Sir John Flamsteed was the first Astronomer Royal and it was in this house that he established accurate measurements of longitude, according to the King's instructions. In the Octagon Room there are clocks with pendulums measuring thirteen feet, which Flamsteed used to measure the rotation of the planet. The galleries are now devoted to permanent exhibitions of time-keeping. This is where Greenwich Mean Time was established. It is also the site of the Meridian; visitors can stand with one foot in each hemisphere.

London City Airport

King George V Dock London E16 2PX
Tel 071-474 5555

The drive to London City Airport is nightmarish, but the airport itself is worth a visit even if you are not flying. It is a neat example of what an inner-city commuter airport *could* be: uncrowded, un-neurotic and efficient. You can park your own car minutes before take-off and walk straight through to a direct flight to European destinations. Steep take-offs on DeHavilland Dash-7s and BAe 146s only for those who like flying.

Financial Times Printing Works

East India Dock Road London E14

An award-winning building by Nick Grimshaw, opened in 1989. New technology allowed the printing operation of the newspaper to be separated from its editorial functions. Line-of-sight microwave dishes connect the remote printworks with the city-based journalists. The architect's bold glass shell allowed the actual mechanics of manufacturing a newspaper to become street theatre, a source of pride for locals and a welcome diversion for lost motorists.

LDDC Storm Water Pumping Station

Stewart Street London E14

For amateurs of post-modernism, John Outram's 1990 creation is an international curiosity with a decadent, Egyptian flavour. Much photographed.

Docklands Sailing Centre

235A Westferry Road London E14 8NX
Tel 071-537 2626

If Docklands does not survive and prosper, this 1989 building by Kit Allsop will be another touching memorial to lost hopes.

Hampstead and the Northwest

Hampstead is a pleasant village on a hill, famed for the suburban cosmopolitanism of its residents (who include an extraordinary number of therapists and psychiatrists, the legacy of Freud and Klein). It has always been an area favoured by *émigrés* of an artistic inclination: Gropius, Mondrian and Moholy-Nagy all stayed here on their way to the United States. It is an area of great charm and small-scale beauty, but there are no *outstanding* shops and restaurants. Rather, genteel Hampstead offers a miniature of the best of contemporary British shopping and formula dining: here you will find branches of Whistles, Waterstones, Café Flo, Oddbins and Ed's Easy Diner. There are many self-conscious pubs.

Isokon Flats

Well Road London NW3

A remarkable 1930s' architectural experiment, by Wells Coates, for 'light travelling aesthetes'. Gropius lived here; Moholy-Nagy was a Hampstead émigré and so was Piet Mondrian, who lived at 60 Parkhill Road. To get a flavour of the period optimism, look at the Connell Ward and Lucas house in Frognal, or Maxwell Fry's nearby Sun House. Down the hill in Camden Town the same firm of architects built a showpiece block of flats in Frederick Street. Michael Ventris, the architect who deciphered the ancient Greek Linear B script, lived at 19 North End. John Constable lived at 40 Well Walk; John Keats lived at Wentworth Place, Keats Grove; D.H. Lawrence lived at 1 Byron Villas, Vale of Health.

Belgo

72 Chalk Farm Road London NW1 8AN
Tel 071-267 0718 Fax 071-267 7508

A cult restaurant of 1992 for jaded north Londoners. It has a Belgian theme and serves a range of Belgian beers with mussels and frites. Waiters winsomely dress as monks.

Freud Museum

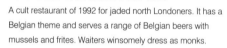

20 Maresfield Gardens London NW3 5SX
Tel 071-435 2002 Fax 071-431 5452

This was Sigmund Freud's last home. The collection of antiquities, rescued from Vienna when Freud settled here in his eighty-second year, suggests the profound influence which the classical past had on Freud's thought. Freud had also told HG Wells that he wanted to become an Englishman, although the atmosphere in this Georgian house is wholly Viennese. The most famous analyst's couch in the world is here, covered with a Turkey rug.

The Underground Café

214 Camden High Street London NW1 8QR
Tel 071-482 0010

Worth eating at, but not worth going to eat at, although it and the **Camden Brasserie 216 Camden High Street London NW1 8QR Tel 071-482 2114** are local favourites.

Au Bois St Jean

122 St John's Wood High Street
London NW8 7SG
Tel 071-722 0400 Fax 071-586 0410

A well-established French restaurant, light on vices and virtues.

Wakaba

122A Finchley Road London NW3 5HT
Tel 071-586 7960

Finchley Road is a hellish stretch of traffic. This is a modish Japanese restaurant designed by John Pawson in his elegant minimalist style. Fine if you are in the area.

Hampstead Heath

Once the forest of Middlesex, now favoured by Hampstead types for deviant versions of softball, or arty walks. Keats and Constable made it famous in verse and paint.

Highgate Cemetery

Swains Lane London NW6 6PJ
Tel 081-340 1834

Highgate is London's spookiest cemetery, famous as the resting place of Karl Marx (in the newer eastern part). There is an Egyptian entrance and catacombs and an altogether fantastic atmosphere of decay.

Islington and King's Cross

Some of London's best domestic architecture is in Islington and contiguous Canonbury. Gracious, dignified, quietly impressive, it is urban development at its very best. Charles Lamb, essayist and author of *Tales from Shakespeare*, lived at 64 Duncan Terrace. Evelyn Waugh was living in Canonbury Square, then in a state of some decrepitude, in 1926 when *Decline and Fall*, the book that made his reputation, was published. The busy Upper Street and the area around Islington Green have plenty of interesting shops and modest restaurants, but few that are exceptional. In his *Memoirs* (1670-1685) Henri Misson said "A Man may spend an hour there agreeably enough. It is not much flock'd to by people of Quality". Fiercely loyal local residents would not agree, but for all its modern interest Islington seems remote from the centre of London.

Camden Passage

London N1

This covered antique market gives the area much of its character. Other shops that fringe the roughly defined boundaries between antiques and junk have spun off into Essex Road. Theberton Street is more genteel. Here you will find **Thomas Asker 11 Theberton Street London N1 0QY Tel 071-226 0626 Fax 071-354 5625** and **D Hassall & Carlow 5 Theberton Street London N1 Tel 071-704 0594**, selling antiques and gifts respectively. **Ruffle & Hook 52 Cross Street London N1 2BA Tel 071-226 0370 Fax 071-359 5798** specializes in fabrics, curtains and blinds.

In the market itself there are hundreds of stalls, but they are nearer *bricolage* than fine art. By the time anything gets to be displayed here it has passed through the hands of many well-weathered dealers. Chance discoveries or freak bargains are not to be expected, which is not to say that a visit here is without charm or delight. On the other side of the busy main road Chapel Street market is more earthy and much less formal, with fewer Volvo wagons and cellphones.

Frederick's

106 Camden Passage London N1 8ED
Tel 071-359 2888 Fax 071-359 5173

Frederick's is an extraordinary place, a living theatre of *trompe-l'oeil,* or so it seems as you pass through an intimate Victorian entrance into a vast and spacious conservatory dining area. The scale of Frederick's as an enterprise means that the food could never, ever hope to be anything better than good mass-catering – and this is exactly what it achieves. Frederick's is not at all intimate, but a pleasing place for an out-of-the-way dinner for a large party.

Upper Street Bookshop

182 Upper Street London N1 2XQ
Tel 071-359 3785

A good second-hand bookshop specializing in the arts.

Gill Wing

194-195 Upper Street London N1 1RQ
Tel 071-359 7697 Fax 071-354 9641

Cards, gifts, jewellery and a cookshop.

Paradox

321 Upper Street London N1 2XQ
Tel 071-226 8530

A modern clothes shop selling the more *outré* celebrity labels, but some lesser known curiosities as well.

The Dressing Room

294 Upper Street London N1 2XQ
Tel 071-354 9955

Offers an unusual retail mix of couture silk wedding dresses and wrought-iron candlesticks.

Upper Street Fish Shop

324 Upper Street London N1 2XQ
Tel 071-359 1401

Middle-class fish and chips, but with ambitious developments into fish soup and pasta. Take your own wine. Environment of right-on proletarian chic.

Casale Franco

134-137 Upper Street London N1 1TQ
Tel 071-226 8994

A courtyard and two floors. Ordinary, but bustling. The popular and decent pizzas are not served at lunchtime, when you have to book, but it's Darwinian in the evening.

Almeida Theatre

Almeida Street London N1 1TA
Tel 071-359 4404 Fax 071-704 9581

A small off-West End theatre with a first-rate reputation for adventurous productions of real quality.

Paula Pryke

20 Penton Street London N1 9PS
Tel 071-837 7336 Fax 071-837 6766

An excellent florist.

Crafts Council

44 Pentonville Road London N1 9HF
Tel 071-278 7700 Fax 071-837 6891

This is the public face of a quasi-autonomous government organization set up to support artist-craftsmen – something it has done with partial success. Since it moved from pricey St James surroundings, the Crafts Council has become

more earnest and more useful. Here you can find interesting
temporary exhibitions, a slide index and a reference library.
The Crafts Council has excellent facilities for sourcing
extravagant jewellery or elaborate jugs that won't pour;
however, no use looking here for a master glazier or tiler.

Anna's Place

90 Mildmay Park London N1 4PR
Tel 071-249 9379

A Swedish restaurant done with conviction, and anything
less would be inappropriate. Somewhat like an Ingmar
Bergman psycho-family nightmare, Anna's Place has an
intrusive sort of intimacy. Swedish 'specialities' served in a
claustrophobically familial atmosphere. There is a reason
why Swedish food has not dominated global cuisine – here
you can find out why. Amusing for the curious.

The **King's Cross** district has yet to develop any very
attractive restaurant or shopping areas, although the part
around the mainline station encourages a notoriously seedy
lowlife. The red light area is only for those with nerve.

Gilbert Scott's glorious **St Pancras Station Euston
Road London NW1 2QP Tel 071-387 7070** (which
a credible myth says was originally a rejected design for the
Foreign Office, which the same architect later built in a
classical style) is the most romantic memorial to the railway
age anywhere. The Gothicky skyline of the station seen
from Pentonville Road at dusk is heartbreakingly beautiful
and painfully redolent of a lost age of optimism.

Great Nepalese

48 Eversholt Street London NW1 1DA
Tel 071-388 6737

In a grim street between St Pancras and Euston stations is
a glorious curiosity, perhaps the only authentic Nepalese
restaurant in London. Nepalese cooking is based on the
principle of fermentation, and there are dishes here whose
taste (and retro-effects) amply demonstrate its perils.

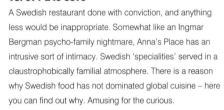

Index

Index